Praise for *The Slab: 2*

"*The Slab* takes episodes fr
beer in this country ... anc
readable way, spiced with s
quirky asides."
Max Allen, *Australian Financial Review*

"A thoroughly entertaining and interesting read -
regardless of whether or not you have any enthusiasm for
beer."
The Crafty Pint

"I loved this book and am confident you will, too."
Roger Hanson, *Hobart Mercury*

"...filled with entertaining anecdotes detailing the role beer
has played in the history of the land Down Under."
Beer & Brewer

"History as it should be written. With beer. About beer"
John Birmingham, author of *Leviathan*

"*The Slab* is a full-bodied book, with a fruity aftertaste
and a nose that carries the slightest hint of sawdust and
vomit. I suggest you XXXX it."
David Hunt, author of *Girt*

ABOUT THE AUTHOR

Glen Humphries is an award-winning beer writer and author of *The Slab: 24 Stories of Beer in Australia*. He is also a journalist at the *Illawarra Mercury*, where he was the movie reviewer for eight years. That meant he got to go to movies during the day and call it work. Yes, he made out it wasn't as easy as it seemed but he was full of crap – get/ting paid to see movies is great. Even the ones with Adam Sandler in them. He was once credited as a tambourine player on a band's CD. He runs the beer blog Beer Is Your Friend (beerisyourfriend.org) and the mirco-publishing site Last Day of School (lastdayofschool.net), where you can purchase all his books. Where does he find the time to raise a family, work full-time, write two blogs and two books? He's not really sure – it just happens. He's @26bear on Twitter, where he has wrapped far too much of his self-worth into getting to 1000 followers. He has never been able to understand why Wonder Woman has an invisible jet when you could see her sitting in it. "Hey, look there's Wonder Woman just sitting in the sky. She must be in her invisible jet." See, total waste of time. To this day he dislikes people if they stand on the right while riding an escalator. He insists on putting dollar notes the right way up in his wallet, and in order of denominations starting with the lowest at the front. As far as the coins go, he just shoves them in his pocket. He Googles his own name far more than is strictly necessary. One day he hopes someone will leave a review on Amazon of one of his books. He wonders if he can get away with saying *The Slab* was nominated for a Walkley Award when he was the one who nominated it. Probably not. He hates exercising but does it so he doesn't feel guilty about skipping it. And also so he doesn't get fat. Well, fatter. He recycles and has a worm farm at home – if the world is going to get wrecked he doesn't want it to be his fault. Fred Flintstone's fat gut was a source of amazement to him. Fred had to power his car with his feet, how come he didn't burn off all that extra weight? He also wrote a stupidly long "About the author" blurb for *The Slab*. It was done to give the reader value for money; you know, fill up what would otherwise be a largely blank page with entertaining stuff to read. If you've made it all the way to this point, he is impressed. Especially considering you've got another 270-odd pages to go.

JAMES SQUIRE

The Biography

GLEN HUMPHRIES

Last Day of School publishing

Aboriginal and Torres Strait Islander people are advised that this publication contains names of people who have passed away.

Copyright Glen Humphries 2017

ISBN: 978-0648032311
James Squire: The Biography is first published in 2017 by Last Day of School
Websites: lastdayofschool.net or beerisyourfriend.org
For more information, to purchase additional copies or just to say how fantastic this book is email dragstermag@hotmail.com. If you hated it, well, that you can keep to yourself.

National Library of Australia Cataloguing-in-Publication entry
Creator: Humphries, Glen, author.
Title: James Squire : the biography / Glen Humphries.
ISBN: 9780648032311 (paperback)
Subjects: Squire, James, 1754-1822.
First Fleet, 1787-1788--Biography.
Convicts--Australia--Biography.
Pioneers--Australia--Biography.
Brewers--New South Wales--Sydney.
Hops industry--Australia--History.

This one's for my parents, who like to tell people "hey, our son wrote a book". Now they can say "hey, he wrote another one".

Acknowledgements

This is my second published book (there are a few manuscripts on the shelves in the study that will likely never see the light of day) and it doesn't get easier.

That's the thing with writing; people seem to think those who publish books have some innate talent. Really the thing you need most is discipline; the ability to sit in front of a computer and bash words onto the screen when you'd really rather be doing anything else. And guilt helps too; it's hard to fob off doing work on the book when you know you'll feel bad about it later.

The planning and publishing side of things was easier the second time around because I knew what I was doing. But the writing? Well, that never gets easier. So if you're a budding writer and you're finding it difficult, then don't worry. That just means you're doing it right.

As with my last book, *The Slab*, the first person to thank is my wife Kim for giving me the space to hide away and type for hours almost every weekend, and for being understanding about the need to do it. And also for her efforts in proofreading this book. Thanks also go to our daughter Josie, for her incredible ability to amuse herself with the iPad while I was writing this book.

My sister Amy allowed me to borrow her stellar proofing skills when I couldn't face having to read through my own book for the sixth time.

Squire researcher and descendent of the guy himself James Donohue went above and beyond the call when some guy he'd never heard of started emailing him with random questions.

Along the same lines, John Boyd from the Fellowship of the First Fleeters was a great help at the start when I needed a bit of confirmation that I was on the right track.

Kate Shepherd served as cover designer again and turned my garbled instructions into a great cover. I think I owe her another case of beer.

Nick O from Crafty Pint, Max Allen in the *Australian Financial Review* and Roger Hanson from the *Hobart Mercury* all wrote nice things about my first book. Thank you one and all for that.

Last but not least, thank you to all those people who bought a copy of *The Slab*. It's good to know there are people out there who like reading about beer.

GLEN
Wollongong
November 2017

"The convicts began to take on an official importance in the great open-air experiment of Sydney that they could not have achieved in Newgate or on the hulks."

Thomas Kenneally
The Commonwealth of Thieves

CONTENTS

<u>Hello</u>

In which we introduce Mr James Squire

There is something worth knowing right here at the start before you go any further – James Squire was a real person.

It was at a family gathering not long after I started working on this book that I realised the fact Squire once lived and breathed wasn't common knowledge. At the get-together I mentioned to my brother-in-law that I was writing a biography of James Squire. He looked at me confused. Which is exactly the sort of thing you'd do if someone had just told you they were writing a biography about a person who wasn't real.

My brother-in-law thought James Squire was a creation of some marketing guy – because of the modern-day line of beers that bear his name and tell a not-always-accurate version of his life story. He thought that they created a man who never was. So it occurred to me that maybe my brother-in-law wasn't alone – maybe there are loads of people out there who think this James Squire character has just been made up to flog beer.

Well, I can assure my brother-in-law – and anyone else who carries that misconception – James Squire is very, very real. Well, he *was* very real; nowadays he's very, very dead. If you've ever walked along Circular Quay in Sydney on the way to catching a ferry or hauled your body up and down the undulating maze of streets that is The Rocks, you've likely stood where James Squire stood (yeah, there was no concrete, paved roads or footpaths in his day, but you know what I mean).

James, an English publican busted for stealing chickens, came out on the First Fleet and, near as I can tell, would have had his tent – and later a proper home – set up in the vicinity of The Rocks. That is where the male convicts were located, with the women on the eastern side and the soldiers in the middle in a forlorn attempt to keep the two apart. Though the soldiers themselves weren't above a nocturnal wander through the female convicts' encampment. A wander, it should be said, that was often quite welcomed by the female convicts.

If you've ever had cause to head up the Parramatta River and gotten off at the Kissing Point terminal, you're also in James Squire territory. After he'd served his convict sentence and became a free man, Squire set up a brewery, pub and a farm in what is now known as the Sydney suburb of Ryde.

There is a paper trail that shows Squire was a living, breathing figure during most of the first 30-odd years of the settlement of Sydney Cove. His name appears in the court records in the early years of the settlement at Sydney Cove – twice as a defendant and at least once as a witness. He is mentioned in the diary of Ralph Clark (a soldier, misogynist and failed purchaser of Aboriginal children) makes regular appearances in the *Sydney Gazette*, the newspaper of the colony and just a few years before his death he gives evidence to a government inquiry into the colony – which is where we get almost all our knowledge of his brewing practices.

While the story wrapped around the beers that bear his name does include some embellishment, there is also some truth there. He really did get flogged for theft in Sydney Cove (though almost certainly got more than 150 lashes), he didn't seem to have great trouble finding a lady (it's worth remembering that, in the early days of the settlement, men greatly outnumbered women) and he was at one stage paid to enforce the law as a police constable.

But, as you're about to find out, some of the Squire story you've learned from beer labels isn't true. Why they had to make up anything strikes me as odd because Squire's life wasn't short of interesting events.

Hello Again

In which we draw an important distinction between James Squire and the beer brand that bears his name

It needs to be said that this a book about the man James Squire and not the brewery that bears his name. But it's worthwhile talking briefly about the beer brand, because that's the first – and possibly only – thing people think of when they hear the name "James Squire".

The brand came about in the late 1990s and was said to have come from a concept put forward by a marketing company, complete with mocked-up beer bottles bearing the James Squire logo. That would suggest the branding came before the beer.

In 1998 a brewery in the Sydney suburb of Camperdown was rebranded the Malt Shovel Brewery, inspired by the real Squire's Malting Shovel Tavern. From there a series of beers were launched with labels that played off aspects of the life of James Squire, sometimes telling the story accurately, sometimes not so much. Over time, the way the beers and the brand have been marketed has changed from being a tribute to James Squire to claiming a non-existent link between the man and the brand. The marketing has gone so far as to actually claim his life story as their own. And I mean that quite literally. As late as November 2017, the beer brand's website boasted a link tagged "Our Story".

Clicking on that link didn't give you the story of the Malt Shovel Brewery based in Camperdown in 1998. What you get is the story of the real James Squire – who has nothing to do with the beers named for him. A man who had been in the ground for more than 150 years when those first beer kegs with "James Squire" stencilled on them rolled out of the Camperdown brewhouse. A man who never even brewed at Camperdown.

This blurring of the historical lines also shows up in advertising, where posters in bottle shops claim their beer is "from Australia's first brewer". Umm, James Squire hasn't brewed beer since the early 1800s; if that beer in the bottle shop is really from him then it's bloody old and will taste awful.

Before I started to work on this book, I believed the stories that were told on the beer labels. But now

I can see some of them are marketing exercises, where the truth gets stretched in order to sell more beer. With all the research I've done for this book, that doesn't sit right with me. I've since developed a liking for the man who was named James Squire, with all his strengths and flaws. So much so that I actually feel a little protective of him, and don't feel comfortable when aspects of his life are altered. And, let's face it, if you're going to use a real person's story to sell a product, there surely has to be a responsibility to make sure the story is correct.

That said, the beer brand has meant the name of the convict-done-very-good has lived on. Without it, Squire would have been nothing more than a footnote in history, a name known only to a few beer geeks with an interest in Australia's past. Speaking as a beer geek with an interest in our past, it's hard to totally knock someone who has highlighted a figure from Australia's history and made his name known to thousands of people. Even if they don't know that he was real.

Because of these beers, I reckon more Australians have heard of James Squire than of Edmund Barton, who was our first Prime Minister. Nothing like beer to make a bit of history a little more interesting.

Also, some of those James Squire beers are quite nice.

Introduction
Let's Go

In which we find out that researching the life of a man who didn't keep a diary is hard work

James Squire was a very busy man indeed. He was a convict, brewer, publican, property tycoon, farmer, husband, father, de facto partner, copper and man who got really pissy at people cutting down trees on his land. So maybe it's not really that surprising that he didn't have much time to keep a diary like any number of other people in the early years of Sydney Cove.

As a result we don't have much from Squire in his own words. There's only his evidence from a government enquiry, where he talks about his beer-making, and the public notices he placed in the *Sydney Gazette* (which is how we know about his aversion to people lopping down his trees).

This means we have to rely on Squire doing things that others found interesting enough to write about. Fortunately, he did enough of those things – good and bad – that people took notice. Most of these occur after he's a free man and the *Sydney Gazette* sees fit to mention his name as often as it can; though, curiously, the paper never carries a single ad for his brewery and pub. Before then, the man pops up on the historical radar much less frequently.

Which does make sense, you have to admit. Remember, these days we have that beer brand that makes it seem like Squire was a really big deal, a super-cool guy who cut a swathe through Sydney Cove and rubbed shoulders with the high and mighty. Now, we all know about James Squire so it's easy to make the mistake that it was always the case. But for so much of his life Squire was really a nobody, just one more person eking out a living in an English town, one more body crammed below the deck of a convict ship, one more criminal getting whipped for breaking the rules.

It would have been great for someone in a time-travelling DeLorean to turn up in the colony of Sydney, point to James Squire and say "hey, that guy is going to be really well-known in about 200 years, you should start writing down everything he does". But there are no reports of Marty McFly turning up in 1788, so no one thought to take any notes of those early years. And really, who could blame them? The guy was just a chicken thief – as if he was going to amount to anything. On top of this, the colonists were too busy trying to stay alive to worry about keeping copious notes on some prisoner who largely seemed to be keeping his head down and not making waves.

And so we have a life with gaps in it. Gaps which people have filled in by either taking educated guesses or sometimes seemingly adopting the not-very-helpful-at-all approach of "making shit up". What's the difference? Well, the former involves taking two known moments in history and drawing a line of best fit between the two which seems reasonable. The latter is where you take a frigging crazy leap based on little or no evidence and come to a conclusion that causes the sober-minded researcher or reader to say "hey, that sounds like it could be bullshit".

I'm probably going to be as guilty of that as anyone on the former but will do my best to flag when I'm taking an educated guess. And when it comes to things that are historically correct, I'll also try and point out where that information comes from. I'll also flag when evidence is a bit sketchy and when someone else's claim made my bullshit detector go off.

Speaking of bullshit, I aimed to avoid the "making shit up" route altogether. Because, what would be the point of that? I don't buy a book of history expecting the author to engage in flights of fancy and I'm sure you don't either.

When it comes to writing about a period in history, there is never one single story. Now that may seem strange to you; after all, history is a collection of things that happened, how can you get more than one story out of that? Well, if that's how history was told then we'd only have one book about World War II. But we don't have one book – we have hundreds. Maybe even thousands. The further we get from that war the more books seem to get written about it. We even end up with books touting themselves as a "new history" of the war.

Writing about history makes me think of a mixing desk in a recording studio. The desk is made up of a series of channels, each with a separate part of the song – vocals, guitar, bass, drums, backing vocals, flute (if it's a prog rock song) – recorded on it. All the parts of the song are there but by sliding one channel up and another one down (sometimes down to zero so it disappears in the mix – goodbye, flute) the producer of the recording can make different versions of the song.

It's the same with writing history – the writer has all the moments that make up the event on separate channels and it's up them to choose which ones to bring up in the mix and which to push to the background. Which ones seem to be significant, defining moments and which ones just get added because they're kind of amusing (early tip: wait to see what Squire's horse was called).

As well as Squire's own story, I've chosen to bring forward the stories of some other convicts and Aboriginal people in Sydney Cove. Sometimes that's because they play a part in Squire's life and other times because I simply find their story interesting. Also, I think it's important not to view Squire in isolation but to look at what else was happening around him. Sometimes, when you pull the focus back, you see things others have missed.

1
We're a Happy Family

In which we find run-ins with the law weren't entirely unknown to James Squire's family

It appears that James Squire wasn't the first member of his family to get in trouble with the law. When he was born on December 18, 1754, to parents Timothy Squires and Mary Wells (yes, the family once had an S at the end of their surname. It wouldn't disappear until long after Squire arrived in Australia. See, you're learning already), London society had just been both titillated and outraged by a scandal that involved a 19-year-old servant named Elizabeth Canning. It's a crime that has rippled through the intervening 260-odd years as true-crime buffs ponder just what happened to that teenage girl in January 1753.

The two women alleged to have done wrong by Elizabeth were Susannah Wells and an old crone by the name of Mary Squires. The smarter reader will have already noted that these two share the surnames of James' parents. Some researchers reckon that this pair were indeed related to James – Mary Squires as his great grandmother while Susannah Wells was a much younger relative on his mother's side.

While finding any direct evidence of that link is difficult – family trees for Squire around this time are hard to come by – the fact the two key miscreants in this caper carry the surnames of Squire's parents seems to be a bit more than a coincidence.

Besides, the Canning Affair is a great story (if you bought my first book, *The Slab*, and read the bit about this case, rest assured what follows is far from a straight rehash).

On New Year's Day 1753 Canning was out and about with her aunt and uncle and, at 9pm she decided to return to her lodgings, next-door to where her mother and four siblings lived – her father had died two years earlier. But she never arrived. Her siblings were sent out to look for her but no trace was found. Her mother continued to search the neighbourhood, notices were placed in newspapers and prayers for her safe return were uttered in churches.

Someone up there must have been listening, for on January 29, almost a month after she disappeared, Elizabeth Canning turned up at her mother's doorstep dirty and bedraggled. She brought with her a horrifying story to tell. She claimed two men had kidnapped her and held her hostage the entire time she had been gone.

She said the men had robbed her and then knocked her unconscious. When she came to, the men forced her to walk to a house, where an occupant – an old lady – looked to turn her into a prostitute. She said that wasn't a vocation she was at all interested in and then, for that intransigence Elizabeth was held captive for a month until managing to escape by kicking a hole in a wall.

Based on a description of the house Canning had given, family members traipsed the area and guessed it was the house of Susannah Wells. Also living in that house was Mary Squires, who was believed to have been rather painful on the eye; in her book on the case Judith Moore wrote that "all accounts do agree that she was an exceptionally ugly woman with a large nose and a lower lip swollen and disfigured by scrofula" (to save you Googling it, scrofula is a form of tuberculosis that causes severe swelling of the lymph nodes). Given James' later success with the ladies it would appear his looks came from his mum's side of the family.

While the case was being investigated, a group of Canning's supporters conducted their own enquiries and also set about raising funds for the girl's legal case. Part of the fundraising involved selling a pamphlet outlining the crime and the offenders, which helped fuel interest in the case. And one would suggest also helped people to find Wells and Squires guilty well before their trials.

Both Wells and Squires denied any involvement in Canning's kidnapping but it did them no good. Wells was charged with "keeping a disorderly house", which doesn't mean she was lazy and left clothes on the floor and dishes in the sink but rather was a polite way of saying she was running a brothel. Squires got the sharp end of the stick, ending up facing a charge of theft – which was punishable by death.

The courts moved much faster in those days, and the case against Wells and Squires began at the Old Bailey on February 21, less than a month after Canning returned home and started telling stories.

In her evidence, Canning said on her way home at 9pm on New Year's Day, she was accosted by "two lusty men, both in greatcoats". One stole some of her clothes and then stuffed a handkerchief in her mouth to silence her scream. "Then they tied my hands behind me; after which one of them gave me a blow on the temple, and said 'damn you, you bitch, we'll do for you by and by'."

Canning then fainted, regaining consciousness near the house she said was Susannah Wells'. She testified that when she was dragged into house, "I saw the gypsy woman Squires, who was sitting in a chair, and two young women in the same room ... Mary Squires took me by the hand and asked me if I chose to go their way, saying, if I did, I should have fine clothes. I said no".

Then she said Squires took out a knife and Canning felt her throat was about to be cut. But Squires just cut her stays (aka undergarments) off her body and took them away, but not before slapping the 19-year-old across the face.

Canning said she was then placed in a room at the bottom of the stairs, which had a pitcher full of water and 24 pieces of bread. Yeah, she's been kidnapped, threatened with a knife and now held hostage but she thought it important to count the pieces of bread. That bread and a small mince pie she had in her pocket was all that Canning claimed she ate or drank during her four-week period of captivity. If you're starting to think Canning's story sounds dodgy, you might be right.

By her own admission, Canning only once bothered to check if the door to the room was locked. She waited four weeks to try and escape, by breaking down a board that was nailed up along the side of the window that was at least three metres off the ground and then climbed out. "First I got my head out, and kept fast hold by the wall and got my body out. After that I turned myself round and jumped into a little narrow place by a lane with a field behind it."

Then she walked all the way to her parents' house, not once stopping anyone along the way for help. Or even food.

Under cross-examination, she said she didn't touch the bread or the water in her room for the first three weeks of her captivity, a fact that prompted the delicate question of "where she did her occasions". She replied that she only had cause to go Number Ones while in the room.

Virtue Hall, who claimed to be in the room with Mary Squires when Canning was first brought in, confirmed the teen's story about being asked to "turn whore" and stating that she was the one who found the girl had escaped.

Mary Squires – named as a fortune teller by a Crown witness – said nothing in her own defence but called up John Giben to offer an alibi that she had been at his inn named The Old Ship from January 1-9. A second witness, William Clarke, said he had also seen her at The Old Ship.

Wells insisted she had never seen Canning before she was arrested and had only laid eyes on Squires a week before that. Given that Squires was apparently as ugly as sin, you'd expect people would remember the first time they saw her.

When you look at them, Canning's description of the events are truly shaky – the idea she ate or drank nothing for three weeks and managed not to be dead as a result is ludicrous; as is the suggestion that, after being held hostage for four weeks, she escaped but asked no one for help on a six-hour journey to her parents' house.

But the jury didn't care; both Wells and Squires were found guilty. Squires was sentenced to death while Wells was to be branded on the thumb and sent to Newgate prison for six months. The odd thing was neither woman was found guilty of Canning's kidnapping and imprisonment; Wells was punished for running a brothel while Squires was sentenced to swing from a rope for stealing Canning's undergarments. At the time, the courts viewed matters like assault and imprisonment as civil issues; if Canning wanted justice for being stuck in a room for a month, she'd have to go after it herself.

Squires would have been a dead woman were it not for trial judge Sir Crisp Gascoyne, who had been in the court listening and felt the verdict stunk to high heaven. He was no fan of Canning's supporters either, whom he felt had intimidated witnesses outside the court and generally acted like a bunch of sanctimonious zealots. He began his own investigation of the case. He soon found out Crown witness Virtue Hall had committed perjury after being threatened with being sent to jail as a felon. He had also spoke to defence witnesses – both those who had appeared and those who did not after being threatened by the so-called "Canningites" – and concluded it was unlikely Squires was anywhere near the area at the time of the alleged crime.

Gascoyne ordered Canning arrested for perjury in March 1793 and wrote to King George II to ask for a stay of execution for Squires. The king gave Squires some breathing room and she would ultimately be pardoned by May of that year. Wells wasn't so lucky – her thumb had already branded and she had already served her six-month sentence by the time of Gascoyne's intervention.

When things turned against her, Canning had remained hidden away, thwarting any attempt to arrest her for perjury. Perhaps finally realising the jig was up, she handed herself in to the law in February 1754. Her perjury trial began on April 29, 1754, and would continue for several days in May. It took a jury just a day to sentence Squires to death, but to work out if someone was lying took six days – that's a weird sense of priorities, huh?

In her perjury case, questions were raised about Canning's description of the room she spent four weeks in and the curious fact that it didn't seem to match any room in Wells' house. Also they called bullshit on the idea she survived for a month on nothing more than a loaf of bread and a pitcher of water. It didn't end well for Canning; the jury found her guilty of perjury and her sentence would be seven years' transportation to the United States.

The guilty verdict sparked anger from her pain-in-the-arse supporters, some of whom apparently threatened the crew of the ship scheduled to take her to America in August. The Canningites arranged for her to live with a minister in Connecticut, not as a servant but as a family member. She would marry John Treat in 1756, give birth to three sons and a daughter before dying suddenly in 1773, aged just 39.

The case, however, continues to intrigue people this day, largely due to the curiosity over what actually happened to Canning for those four weeks in January 1753. Some believe she really was held hostage as a result of protecting her virtue, while others think she did indeed become a whore for that period and made up the whole kidnapping story to keep her horizontal employment a secret.

Another theory has it that her disappearance was in order to hide a pregnancy, or that she was indeed held captive but just not in Wells' house.

Or maybe she was an amnesiac who did not knowingly lie at the trial of Wells and Squires. The most interesting theory is the "fugue state" option put forward by author Lillian de la Torre in her novel based on the case.

De la Torre posits that Canning was kidnapped at the behest of a man who wanted to keep her as his mistress. On her first night, the man rapes her, which pushes Canning into a fugue state – a temporary sort of amnesia.

The man tires of her and then hands her off to Wells, who doesn't know what to do with the girl. So she puts her in the spare room. Then, in late January, Canning awakens from her state and quickly escapes. Perhaps on her walk back to her parents' she creates a story to explain, to herself as much as anyone else, just what happened to her.

And so when she testifies in court she is committing perjury but, confusingly for her, she believes herself to be telling the truth.

2
Stand and Deliver

In which we wonder whether James broke the law before being sent off to Australia

For the first two decades of Squire's life, there doesn't seem to be a whole lot of information left to us. It seems he was the eldest of three children – he had a brother five years younger than him named Timothy and a sister, Mary, who was 10 years younger. There was, apparently, an elder brother also named Timothy who was born in 1751 – three years before Squire, but we can assume he probably died as a baby, hence the second Timothy. Either that or his parents were really lacking in imagination when it came to coming up with names for their kids.

Squire doesn't make any real appearance on the radar until 1774. This is when, according to one story, he runs out of a freshly-ransacked house with some unspecified loot in hand. As he leaves, he runs straight into the fuzz, who arrest him. But, luckily for Squire, he left by the front door which opened onto the highway, so he was charged with highway robbery rather than the more serious charge of stealing.

Now look, this tale may well be true but, to me, it sounds decidedly dodgy. I could find not a shred of contemporary evidence, no charge sheet, no mention of a court appearance. It may well be that the paperwork for this case sits in a dusty box in some suburban British library. But I don't have the cash – or enough leave points built up with the wife – to fly to Britain to ferret around for something that may or may not be there.

It is telling, however, that no secondary source I have seen quotes directly from this charge sheet. Instead, every reference to this event I found – even those published in books – seems to be using the same original source which contains not a whit of contemporary evidence.

What makes me skeptical is the idea that Squire got off lightly by being charged with highway robbery rather than stealing.

My reading of this period leads me to conclude highway robbery was far from the lesser of the two charges. Indeed there was a time when both it and stealing were punishable by death (which isn't saying much. In the late 1770s the British would kill criminals for all sorts of things. If cars were around in those days it's likely drivers who failed to use their indicators when turning would be strung up). Additionally, highway robbery was in itself a serious offence at the time as it was viewed as a restraint on trade and stopped the free flow of the gentry going from town to town to look down upon the peasants. If he was ever charged with something related to the theft, being in possession of stolen goods would seem far more likely as it would see him avoid swinging from the end of a rope.

Incidentally, suggesting that running out the front door and straight into the arms of the cops was a lucky break is bizarre. To me, it seems that if he ran out the back door he would have avoided the cops altogether and got away with whatever was in his hessian sack stencilled with the word "Loot" (okay, so maybe that's the sort of thing only cartoon crooks use).

Anyway, what apparently happens next is the judge finds Squire guilty (of something or other) and sentences him to seven years' transportation to America. Squire is somehow able to change that to joining the British Army and serving in America.

This does seem a little curious to me. At the time,

sending convicts to America was a no-brainer for the Brits. It was dirt cheap for the government to fling convicts over there. They just paid a merchant with a boat a few pounds per convict and, once the contract was signed and the human cargo handed over, the government's responsibility – financial or otherwise – was over. After that the merchant would sell the convict's labour to the US settler with the highest bid.

Compare this to a soldier in the British army, for whom the government needed to cover the ongoing expenses of food, clothing, shelter and transportation. Opting to put Squire in the army rather than in chains seems far and away the more expensive option for the British. Unless they figured he would be so hopeless as a soldier that he'd get shot inside a few weeks and therefore not cost them as much.

I've not seen any direct evidence that Squire served in any military, though it does explain later references to him in Australian newspapers of the 1880s as a "former soldier" or a "time-expired soldier" – this pre-transportation period of Squire's life is the most likely time for him to have served in the military. Also, once in Australia Squire becomes the servant of a lieutenant in the marines, who trusts the convict enough to give him a rifle and protect him while he chats to the Aborigines. To me, that action makes more sense if

Squire was a former soldier – the lieutenant may well have seen another military man and felt he could be trusted enough not to shoot him in the back.

Somehow, Squire is able to leave America and return home in 1776 – right around the time when the American revolution is kicking off. That's where the Americans say to the British "you're not the boss of me" while the British respond with "check out the globe suckers, we're the boss of everyone". Queue much gunfire, chucking of tea into the Boston harbour and George Washington presumably saying "this is our Independence Day" (after all, if anyone has the right to say that, it's him).

Even though there is a war on Squire manages to get sent home. It is unlikely to be because he was seriously injured in some battle as not one source from the First Fleet onwards makes any mention of Squire missing a limb or having some other serious war injury.

One thing we do know for a fact is Squire has to be back in Britain by 1776 because that's when the 22-year-old marries Martha Quinton, who is the same age. Precious little is known of her, though if Squire did go to America, presumably he knew her before he left. It appears they were married in Kingston-upon-Thames, the same town in which Squire grew up. So perhaps

Quinton grew up there too and they had known each other for years.

They had three children together – John (born in 1778), Sarah (1780) and James (1783). Years later, in the new colony of Sydney, Squire would see fit to recycle the names of his two youngest British-born children when naming those he fathered on Sydney soil.

The family, like many in Britain of the later 1700s, weren't exactly swimming in cash. Money was certainly tight but, by 1777, according to Mollie Gillen's book *The Founders*, Squire was living in Heathen (now Eden) Street in his home town of Kingston-Upon-Thames, which is around 20 kilometres south-west of London

There is some suggestion Squire was managing a hotel in Heathen Street which, if is true, likely means the family was living over the hotel – or very close to it. It could also likely mean Squire was meeting some customers of dubious character, which may have influenced him to make a decision that would split apart his family and, surprisingly, change his life for the better.

3
I Don't Like Mondays

In which we wonder whether Squire was an unlucky guy, a career criminal or framed. Yes, hypothetical arguments can be fun

If Squire was a chick flick fan he may well have viewed the events of Monday April 11, 1785, as a sliding doors moment. If you don't get that chick flick reference I totally understand. *Sliding Doors* was a film starring Gwyneth Paltrow and, really, no one needs to remember any of her films. Not even that one where she won an Oscar for a level of hammy acting not seen from anyone who isn't Porky Pig. Basically this day was when one door closed for Squire but another opened.

That Monday in April 1785 was the day the law came down on Squire. At the incredibly longwindedly named General Sessions of the Peace for the Town and Hundred of Kingston upon Thames he was sentenced to seven years' transportation. His crime, was highway robbery, and his haul was "four cocks, five hens and divers [and] other goods and chattels the property of John Stacey". Yeah, he stole some chickens. According to Gillen's *The Founders*, this Mr Stacey had just moved into Heathen Street, which meant Squire had ripped off his neighbour. That's not a smart move at the best of times, let alone when you've swiped an animal that likes to crow all the time.

Stacey: Good morning, James. I hear you've got some roosters in the backyard.

Squire: Umm, yes.

Stacey: That's an interesting coincidence, for until recently I too had some roosters in my backyard. Funny how I lost mine at exactly the same time you got yours.

Squire: Yes, yes it is. Hey, John, look over there. [Squire runs away]

Much has been made of Squire's astonishingly bad luck when it comes to committing crime. He does it twice (including the 1774 charge) and gets pinged both times. But stop to think about this for a minute. Doesn't it seem a little odd for Squire to commit just two crimes a decade apart? Doesn't it seem weird that, one day in April, Squire just out of the blue decides to steal some chickens? If you ask me, the answer to those questions is yes. We only know of these two instances (assuming the first charge even happened) because he was nabbed and appeared in court. An absence of any charges in the years between 1774 and 1785 isn't proof that he committed no other crimes. Indeed, it's just as likely that he committed other crimes in that period but was never caught.

Maybe I'm a bit of a skeptic but I lean towards the latter possibility; that Squire could have been guilty of more than just the two crimes we know of. He was managing an inn for a number of years that was reportedly the home of smugglers and other dodgy types. Keeping that sort of company makes it a bit hard to swallow that Squire managed to keep his nose clean for a decade and then woke up one morning and decided "bugger it, I'm going to steal my neighbour's chooks".

The idea that he committed only two crimes in his life, separated by a decade, and was so incredibly unlucky as to get busted both times is also a bit hard to swallow.

To be fair, someone could also spin the story in another direction such is the nature of the gaps in Squire's life. He and Martha's third child, James was born on May 2, 1783, two years before the chicken thievery. Maybe the family had been able to get by when there were four mouths to feed but, when little James comes along, pressure comes to bear on the family finances.

Maybe Squire swipes the neighbour's chickens out of a desperate need to feed his family. Perhaps it was the latest in a series of petty thefts committed since James' arrival and Squire got away with those because he wasn't boneheaded enough to commit them in his own street.

Absent of any court testimony or Ouija board explanation from Squire about his motives, you could go all-out and mount a case for him being stitched up. As we will be able to deduce from Squire's later successes in Sydney Cove, he is clearly not a totally stupid man. Out of nothing, he managed to build up quite the colonial empire. Were you to put forward the "Squire is innocent" claim, you might well suggest that only a stupid man commits a crime in the very street in which he lives. Perhaps Squire was a patsy for some chicken thief that has disappeared into the fog of history.

But, if you ask me, I reckon Squire might have pinched a bit more stuff than we know about.

Something Squire and his family wouldn't have known on that dark Monday in 1785 was just where he would be sent. While a sentence of transportation was handed down, there would have been no destination on his boarding pass.

The war in America had put on hold the British penchant of shovelling the dregs of their society across the Atlantic. Between 1650 and 1775, according to Thomas Keneally in his book *The Commonwealth of Thieves*, the Brits punted as many as 120,000 convicts to America (though other sources do suggest a lower figure than that).

Using America as a jail had been working well for the British, largely because it cost them bugger-all and the crims ended up as someone else's responsibility. In his book, *Botany Bay: The Real Story*, Alan Frost says the government foisted off the responsibility of transporting the convicts to third parties, paying them £5 per convict and then washing their hands of any further obligation. "[Transportation] was essentially a private business," Frost writes, "for the role of central government ceased once merchants had signed contracts and taken custody of the convicts".

Still, the merchants saw the convicts as a way to make money, because their labour would be sold at auction on arrival. The average going rate for a male convict was £10 while a woman could fetch a merchant £9. Those younger men with skills like carpentry or blacksmithing could go for £15 to £25.

Sometimes the chance to make elephant bucks was so easy that the merchants told the government it could forget about the £5 per prisoner fee, they'd take them for free. "… At times, when the demand for labour was strong in the colonies," Frost writes, "the merchant might transport the convicts for no fee, knowing he could cover his costs and make a profit by selling the labour of his charges at a higher than usual rate".

From the mid-1770s, the British government was fishing around for another place to dump their detritus. They considered Gibraltar and an area along the Senegal River in Africa. They also considered another location in West Africa called Lemane, somewhere in Canada or the West Indies. This place called New South Wales that Captain James Cook had discovered was briefly considered but rejected because, unlike shipping the convict scum to America, sending them to Australia would cost too much.

In the meantime, the government passed laws that allowed those sentenced to transportation to be moved from prisons to ships – which were called hulks – moored in the Thames, in sight of Londoners, as well as at Plymouth and Portsmouth. It seems this was a bit of a PR exercise, a way of saying to the populace "See, we've gone and put them on the boats and as soon as we find a place to send them, they're out of here. Honest". Yet it didn't work out that way for, unsurprisingly, Londoners didn't like boatloads of convicts living just a brief longboat paddle away. Funny that.

Finally, in August 1786 – more than a year after Squire was sentenced – he found out he was heading halfway around the world to this place called Sydney Cove (because the English had run out of other options). A place so far away that no English person had visited it since Captain Cook in 1770. Despite just one visit nearly two decades earlier, the British figured they'd send them there. "It might cost us a bit," they may have said, "but at least they'll be a long, long, long way from here. With any luck, maybe most of them will be eaten by cannibals. We know there are black people living there and all black people are savages and cannibals, unlike us civilised white folk."

Despite his sentence of transportation, Squire wasn't on any of the hulks parked in the Thames. He had been locked up in Southwark jail since the courts had passed judgement on him. And the prisons in England at the time were weird, weird places.

For starters, they often weren't run by the government but licenced to private operators. And those operators could charge prisoners a sliding scale of fees. Those fees including "extras" like food, bedding or even the removal of leg irons. Oh, and beer too.

Some prisons had a taproom where the licencee would sell inmates a beer if they had the cash. Prison reformer John Howard found that, in one jail, the landlord had sublet the taproom to one of the prisoners, who was doing a roaring trade.

According to Tom Keneally, the English at the time viewed prisons as a bit of a tourist attraction, as a place to go to see how the other half lived and to revel in the vicarious thrill that you weren't them. A low-rent Disneyland, if you will.

"Every day, sightseers came to view the spectacle, as we might now visit a zoo, while prostitutes worked their way around to service visitors and prisoners who had the cash, and turnkeys received a pay-off from this traffic as well."

Prisons were not just weird places, but awful ones as well. Reformer Howard described cells measuring five metres by 1.8 metres housing at least two dozen inmates with nothing more than a few holes in the door to provide air and light. After some visits,

Howard said his notebook was so tainted by the fetid stench of the prisons that he had to lay the pages out before the fire to dry and disinfect them.

The jail system seems almost enough to make transportation to a country no Englishman had been to for more than a decade look attractive by comparison. Well, except for the fact that they had to say goodbye to their families and everything they knew – most likely forever – and journey to this strange land a long, long way away. The modern Australian has no qualms about travelling to and from our country. But it was a very different story for the people who would become the first Australians (okay, the first *white* Australians). Their journey from England to Australia has been described as the 18th century equivalent of going to Mars, and that's pretty close to the money. Leaving the familiar – even if it's the familiarity of a stinking jail or overcrowded hulk in The Thames – to journey to a place almost no one in England had been to would surely have seemed like a step into the unknown.

But it was one Squire wouldn't have to make on his own.

4

Jailhouse Rock

*In which we get a very quick – and
hopefully accurate – explanation as to why
London seemed to be locking everyone up*

When Squire committed his crimes – both those
that we know about and the ones in between that, let's
face it, are very bloody plausible – he was far from the
only one running foul of the law. Back in the mid to
late 1700s, just about everyone was doing it. Well,
everyone who didn't already have lots of money to
start with, that is.

Hedges and fences were in no small part to blame
for London becoming an apparent hotbed of petty
crime. The mid-1700s brought in something called the
Enclosures Act, where the government chose to fence
in what had previously been common ground in rural
villages. That sucked if you were a poor farmer
because you used that land to do things like grow

crops or graze your animals. But when those fences or hedgerows went up and your access was gone, well, so was your livelihood.

And there was nothing else for it but to go to the city and try your luck there. Just like the shit-heeled farmers from every other village around. You may not be surprised to know that there weren't many well-paying jobs for a rural farmer in the city, and so many of these country hicks who moved to the big smoke would turn to crime to survive. And, perhaps because they were not all that good at it, would find themselves caught and jailed.

Another part of the problem was the end of the war with America. According to Alan Frost in *Botany Bay: The Real Story*, England didn't have a standing army "as prevailing wisdom held that this would be inimical to true English liberty, for it would give a tyrant the means to impose his dictatorship". Yes, far better to unleash a mass of suddenly jobless soldiers and sailors onto England. Yes, that seems like such a better idea.

In fact, Frost says having the army and navy at war in another country helped to curb the crime rate in England.

"During conflict, as rogues were absorbed into the army and navy, the incidence of assaults and property crimes diminished; after it, it rose sharply. Put ashore at the Channel ports, far away from family and friends and with no other means of support, many of the demobilised men soon squandered their pay on women, alcohol and gambling; for such men, the temptation to turn their martial skills to assault and robbery could be irresistible."

And of course there were also those dodgy types that saw population centres as full of potential marks and chose to move there purely for the rich pickings.

Suffice to say, there was no shortage of human cargo that could be shunted onto those First Fleet ships and flung out to some country on the other side of the world.

In fact there were so many convicts it seems the government didn't feel the need to pay close attention to just how many they were sending to Australia. It's almost as though they took the attitude of "well, let's just keep throwing them on board until we run out of room".

Robert Hughes in his book *The Fatal Shore* puts the number of convicts on the First Fleet at 736. Alan Frost reckons there were 750. Tom Keneally in *The Commonwealth of Thieves* says 759 convicts were bound for Botany Bay. I think the lack of care in counting heads and keeping accurate records says something about the purpose of the voyage – to load them in as quickly as possible and get them the hell away from England.

By the way, there is a school of thought that says using Australia as a great big jail a long way away wasn't the sole aim here. That school suggests there was also the idea of beating those pesky French to Australia, taking advantage of the pine trees and flax to make masts and sails for ships (turned out the pine and flax were both rubbish for use on ships) and even seeing it as getting the English foot in the door in terms of trade in the region.

This last one would apparently get the noses of the Dutch out of joint, who liked to keep the trade routes down that part of the world to themselves. So this is why, the school of thought goes, the official government papers on Australia only mention its use as a place to store England's naughty people. It was the Brits being sneaky.

Now, whatever the reason for the settlement of Australia, that doesn't really concern us here (though I reckon it had to be more than just a jail, because sending convicts there was ridiculously expensive. The government would have surely wanted some sort of return on that outlay). Really, all that matters for our purposes is that they sent a bunch of crims to

Australia. And some guy named James Squire was one of them.

5

Six Months in a Leaky Boat

In which we see conditions aboard the First Fleet were so bad one convict couldn't take it anymore

Our man Squire was one of the 71 people on the First Fleet who were done for highway robbery. That's according to the figures Hughes gives in *The Fatal Shore*, and it seems that is the go-to source for early Australia (well, unless you're historian Alan Frost, who describes Hughes as "the art critic whose historical research was inadequate". Yes, even historians have their bitchy side).

The vast majority of convicts – 431 – were done for minor theft. While I couldn't find any evidence of a convict being transported for that oft-cited crime of "stealing a loaf of bread", there were plenty of souls on those ships whose theft was well and truly minor.

A West Indian named Thomas Chaddick stole some cucumber plants, William Francis stole a book (and not a very interesting one either – its title was *A Summary Account of the Flourishing State of the Island of Tobago*), William Holmes, perhaps not born with a silver spoon in his mouth, chose to make up for it by stealing 17 of them. Mary Turner stole a few items of clothing worth no more than £2. John Cross, whose path would cross with Squire's in the Sydney Cove court system, nicked a sheep.

So we can see here that, in terms of the crime committed versus the sentence meted out, Squire's seven years for chicken theft was by no means unusual.

His presence on the First Fleet seems almost an afterthought, a late move to fill a few vacancies on board. With the fleet's departure just two months away and almost all the convicts already onboard, Squire was still in Southwark jail.

On March 10, 1787, he and fellow inmate James Bloodworth (about whom we will hear more of shortly) were mentioned in a dispatch from Evan Nepean, the undersecretary to Home Secretary Lord Sydney, to the Town Clerk at Kingston Upon Thames. "…James Squires and James Bloodworth should be taken to the coast of New South Wales for the times they are sentenced to be transported," the letter reads.

It then goes on to talk about getting the contracts drawn up to allow the transfer of the prisoners from the jail to the master of the Friendship, the First Fleet ship that would take them to a strange new place. The letter closes with a sentence that suggests the pair's addition was a last-minute decision.

"I must beg the favour of you to get the instruments prepared as soon as possible as no time is to be lost in getting the convicts put on board the ships being now upon the eve of their departure."

Well, not quite. The letter was written in March and, as time would tell, the First Fleet wouldn't see England in the rear view mirror until May 13. It would have been May 12 but there was a false start, which has been variously attributed to roaring hangovers or a captain who was a bit of a scammer.

On May 12, Captain Arthur Phillip said "we're outta here" and began to sail off. But, when he looked back, he saw "several of the convoy not getting under way, through some irregularity in the seaman", according to the diary of the fleet's chief surgeon John White.

Phillip sent Lieutenant Philip Gidley King over to see why those ships were pissfarting about. In White's telling, King "soon adjusted the difficulties that had arisen, as they were found to proceed more from intoxication than from any nautical causes." In other words, the sailors' heads were throbbing and they were in desperate need of some Berocca and a hamburger and chips.

It's unclear where White got his information from as King himself would later claim the delay was due to a mini-mutiny. His story would be that the seamen hadn't been paid for months and, not unreasonably, wanted some cash so they could buy things for the trip. The ships' masters, on the other hand, wanted to pay them after they'd set sail so they'd have to buy goods from the ship store at rather inflated prices – which would have lined the pockets of the masters.

Either story could be true. Sailors may well be prone to tie one on the night before a big voyage, and the masters could have been looking at a way to wring a few bucks out of their crew. But King was the one on the ships dealing with the issue, so you'd have to accept his story. Even if the hangover tale is more fun.

The conditions on the First Fleet for Squire and the other convicts would have been quite cramped. To give an appreciation for how small the ships in the First Fleet were, you could pretty much pick any two of the 11 ships and they would fit side by side in an

Olympic swimming pool – without touching the sides, or each other. Sirius, the widest ship in the fleet, was just nine metres wide. As for touching the ends of the swimming pool, forget it – the convict transport Alexander was the longest ship in the fleet and it was only 34 metres long.

Below decks there wasn't a lot of room, with many convicts not being able to stand up straight. On the transport Scarborough the headroom was just 1.3 metres in some places.

"The areas below decks normally assigned to cargo were divided up into cells with the placement of temporary bulkheads and iron grilles," Rob Mundle writes in *The First Fleet*. "Some cells were so small that four men, some of whom wore chains or irons, could barely lie on the floor to sleep, and the toilets were buckets."

The portholes and hatchways were covered, making convict holds as dark as night even in the middle of the day and fresh air was hard to come by. One bright side for the convicts was that Phillip would order the removal of their shackles once the fleet had left England.

There is some confusion as to which ship in the fleet Squire would be found in. That letter from Nepean says he was destined for the Friendship, yet other sources state that when the fleet arrived at Sydney Cove Squire disembarked from the Charlotte.

There is the possibility that both are right. During the journey, the fleet stopped in at the Cape of Good Hope to pick up supplies. Marine and famed First Fleet diarist Watkin Tench lists the purchases made as "…two bulls, three cows, three horses, forty-four sheep and thirty-two hogs, besides goats and a very large quantity of poultry of every kind." On top of that were the animals bought by the soldiers and "a considerable quantity of flour".

Space for supplies was needed in the already-cramped conditions of the ships, and so they played Convict Tetris and moved them around – from the Friendship to the Charlotte. It seems to have been mainly the female convicts, but Squire too could have been part of the reshuffle.

The Squire beer brand gave its IPA the name of Stowaway and likes to tell the story that Squire managed to sneak aboard the women's ship and had a very enjoyable voyage – nudge-nudge wink-wink. Reality doesn't support that story. Firstly, how would Squire, a convict, have managed to leave one ship in the fleet and sneak aboard another without anybody noticing? Are we expected to believe he dove into the water from the deck of the Friendship and managed to swim across to the "women's ship", somehow climb aboard and hide among the ladyfolk without anyone seeing any of his exploits? Oh please, give it a rest.

Secondly, the ship Squire was on already *had* women on board. Yep, the Friendship had 21 female prisoners among its human cargo – which was more than the Charlotte when they left England. So Squire had been in close proximity to women for the entirety of his voyage.

Thirdly, there was just one ship that had only female convicts; that was the Lady Penrhyn. And there is simply no evidence from anyone to suggest Squire was anywhere near that ship.

So Squire never stowed away on any female ship. He was likely moved from one ship carrying some female convicts to another ship that also carried some female convicts.

While Squire didn't dive into the water and swim from one ship to another, the idea of escaping from the First Fleet while in transit really isn't totally implausible. We know this because one convict actually attempted it. John Power got a seven-year sentence to Australia for stealing a tonne of wood. Well, that's a slight exaggeration, it was 52 kilograms short of a tonne. Yep, Power and his partner in crime Charles Young swiped 948 kilograms of wood – red sandalwood, to be specific.

Power was on the convict transport Alexander and decided to make his bid for freedom after less than a month at sea. The fleet docked at Tenerife for supplies on June 3 but he didn't chance his arm until June 8 – maybe he needed to build up the courage for the escape. In his diary surgeon John White says Power used the cover of taking water on board "to drop himself unperceived into a small boat that lay alongside and, under cover of night … cast her off without discovery".

He first floated to a nearby ship from the Dutch East India Company, spun them a tale and begged to be taken on board. They mustn't have believed him; despite being in need of crew members, they turned him away.

"Having committed himself again to the waves, he was driven by the wind and the current," White wrote in his diary, "in the course of the night, to a small island lying to leeward of the ships, where he was the next morning taken."

White reckons he would have been free and clear but for the inability to hide the escape boat and oars, which led to his discovery. Once back on board Phillip put him in chains for a time before an "artful petition" written on his behalf so tugged at the captain's heartstrings that he set Powers free from his chains.

6

When Will I Be Famous?

In which we meet some of the fascinating people our man shared a ship with. Including the other James Squire

These days James Squire is one of the First Fleet's most well-known convicts. Which is a bit unfair because there are loads of other convicts sharing a ship with Squire who should themselves be better-known. Below decks of, at first the Friendship and later the Charlotte, he was surrounded by others who would also make their name in Australia. One would quite literally help build the country while several others would stage an audacious escape from it. One would quickly become a footnote for managing to die within weeks after first setting foot in this strange new land. Another would receive unfortunate renown for being ridiculously young when sentenced to transportation.

Also in chains in the Friendship were two people

whose saga, in this day and age would have set social media ablaze. These would be Susannah Holmes and the red-headed Henry Kable. Kable had been done for burglary but dodged the death sentence while literally standing on the scaffold. According to Gillen's book *The Founders*, he and his cohorts (who included his dad Henry) broke into a house and "stripped it of every moveable, took the hangings from the bedsteads and even the meat out of the pickle casks".

While stuck in Norwich jail, he fell in love with fellow burglar Holmes (she pinched some linen and silver spoons) and the two had a prison child in 1786 named Henry – clearly the Kable family struggled to come up with names for boys.

Baby Henry couldn't accompany his mum and dad down onto the First Fleet and instead was looked after by the Norwich jailer John Simpson. With she on the Charlotte and he on the Friendship, the new family was completely split up.

Something about their plight touched Simpson – or maybe he just didn't want to be stuck looking after someone else's kid. So he started writing letters to those in power. Soon enough the story of the family separated by cruel circumstances caught on with the public and they began to call for the family to be brought together (hashtag "reunited").

It worked; Simpson brought young Henry down to the docks to hand over to Holmes and then she and bub were transferred to the Friendship to be with the Fanta-headed Kable.

The couple would be among the first to get married in Sydney. They would eventually become a prosperous pair, with Kable's dealings allowing them to amass a lot of property. Not all were pleased with the way they did it; Governor John Hunter felt Kable in particular liked to use the law to send the opposition broke; "with constant litigation and infamous prosecutions in the courts, they have been accustomed to be gratified".

Also sharing space with Squire in the bowels of the Friendship was the unfortunate John Hudson, a chimneysweep who was all of nine years old when he was sentenced to seven years transportation in December 1783.

Hudson was convicted of breaking into a house and swiping some shirts, stockings, a pistol and two aprons. He was fingered by the householder, who saw the marks of sooty feet near the window. He took impressions of them with paper and they matched Hudson's in size and so he confessed. Which means, if he had bathed before committing the crime he would have likely gotten away with it.

Hudson was down to be sent to the United States, but the War of Independence put paid to that and so the boy waited on the hulks in the Thames for four years before journeying to Australia at the ripe old age of 15. Once ashore he would be sent to Norfolk Island and the last known record of him was his receiving 50 lashes in February 1791 for being outside his hut after hours. After that, the First Fleet teen largely disappeared from history.

Hudson wasn't the youngest convict on the First Fleet. That honour appears to belong to Elizabeth Hayward, who was 13 years old when she set sail on the Lady Penrhyn.

Also travelling on the Friendship was marine, diarist and devoted misogynist Ralph Clark. He would routinely write about the "damned bitches" that were the female convicts on board – so often in fact he ended up using the shorthand "D/B" to describe them. He would also take on James Squire as a servant for a time in the colony.

When Squire was moved to the Charlotte he was in close quarters with the fleet's other famed diarist, Marine Watkin Tench. Squire mustn't have made much of an impression on either of them – neither Tench nor Clark make any mention of him during the trip over.

The convict lists on the Charlotte were sprinkled with those who would go on to be famous and infamous. Among the famous was James Bloodworth, the convict with whom Squire was added to the fleet at the last minute.

According to historian Mollie Gillen, Bloodworth's parents lived on Heathen Street, the very same street where Squire's pub could be found. So it seems reasonable to assume the pair knew each other before becoming passengers on the First Fleet.

Once in Sydney, Bloodworth found his skills as a bricklayer to be very much in demand. He built a number of the buildings in the colony, including the first Government House which was finished in June 1789 – just over a year after construction began. Once his sentence had finished and he was free to leave, Bloodworth chose to stay in the colony as the master bricklayer.

Perhaps the most infamous of those travelling on the Charlotte was Mary Broad, though she would become known as Mary Bryant soon after landing in Sydney Cove when she married fellow Charlotte passenger William Bryant.

Mary was the brains behind the most audacious escape from Sydney Cove – one which saw them return home to England. While a number of convicts ran off into the bush surrounding Sydney Cove looking for freedom, in March 1791, Mary, William, their two small children (aged just two and three) would steal a small fishing boat and sail away, having stockpiled supplies over the previous months.

Their escape was successful – they had waited until there were no faster ships in the harbour that could catch them. They sailed up the east coast and, after 10 weeks at sea, landed at Timor and posed as survivors of a shipwreck. The Dutch governor there looked after them and, in a delicious irony, Bryant and their party drew bills on the British government to buy clothes and supplies.

The fun was over two months later, when their real identities were discovered. They were handed over to the next English ship and taken back home. Once there Bryant became a minor celebrity and would ultimately be pardoned and released in 1793 – not a bad result for a prison escapee.

Also on the Charlotte was a teen named Thomas Barrett, who was unaware he only had a handful of months left on this Earth. He had already twice dodged a death sentence. His first dodge was when, just 12 years old, he was found guilty of stealing a silver watch. Sentenced to death, it was commuted to transportation to Nova Scotia in 1782. He was to travel there onboard the Mercury, but that ship was taken over by the convicts before it left British waters. Once recaptured, he and the other so-called "Mercuries" were sentenced to death, but again, Barrett's sentence was commuted to transportation – this time to a place called Sydney Cove.

While onboard the Charlotte, Barrett managed to turn a belt buckle and a few old pewter spoons into counterfeit coins so good they very nearly passed undetected. How Barrett managed to melt the metal and recast them into coins while under the watch of marines seemed a mystery – though one of the marines was apparently caught with some of Barrett's handiwork on him, which suggests at least one of those guarding him was prone to turning a blind eye from time to time.

By the time the Charlotte arrived at Botany Bay, the teenaged Barrett would only have weeks to live.

Over on the Lady Penrhyn is where we find a curious thing – another James Squire (though both still had an S appended to the end of their surname). The other Squire was the second mate on the Lady Penrhyn (which might explain the origin of the incorrect claim that the convict Squire ended up on the female ship). While not a convict, this other Squire did get himself in trouble; on April 19, 1787, before the fleet set sail, he was caught sleeping with a female convict. He was one of five seamen caught, quite literally, with their pants down, and all only narrowly avoided being kicked off the fleet.

It seems this other Squire was a seriously odd cat. After his ship had dropped off its load of convicts and left Sydney, it returned via China. On that voyage, he got in trouble for cruel treatment of the captain's Tahitian goat. In one of the strangest cases of revenge you're ever likely to hear about, Squires tied a large stone around the neck of his own dog (yes, *his own* dog) and threw the poor creature overboard.

Finally, if we were to fly over to another ship, the Prince of Wales, we would find the heavily pregnant Mary Spencer. While she and Squire would in time become quite familiar with each other, when the ships crossed the waters, they were strangers.

Sent away for stealing a corset, two handkerchiefs and a cloak, Spencer boarded the Prince of Wales in April 1787, already around five months pregnant. Perhaps the pregnancy was the result of a last clinch with a lover before leaving England or maybe just a jailhouse romance.

She would give birth to baby Mary on July 1, who would only survive three months in Sydney before dying and being buried under the soil of this strange place on April 5, 1788.

7

Taking Care of Business

In which Governor Arthur Phillip discovers he needs a Plan B

It's a safe bet virtually none of the convicts had ever been at sea before their forced eight-month voyage to Sydney. And it would have been an unpleasant experience as well. Even worse than boarding Fairstar the Funship and finding every other ticket has been bought by bogans or park footy players on an end of season trip.

While Phillip had been considerate enough to remove the convicts' chains while at sea, they still must surely have looked forward to the day they arrived so they could get the hell off the damned ship. Maybe they even annoyed the marines with endless refrains of "are we there yet?".

So they were no doubt cranky to finally arrive in Australia only to be told they had to stay on board for another week. There they were, the shoreline of this strange world, perhaps visible through small cracks in the wood in the side of the ship – certainly visible to those who were allowed on deck to go fishing – and yet they had to wait. Well, except for one convict who was good at giving piggyback rides.

Supply was the first ship in the fleet to arrive in Botany Bay on January 18 (at 2.15pm, if you need to know). Arthur and some of the marines wasted little time in getting ashore; they hoisted a few longboats into the water and rowed to the shore. Convict James Ruse was in one of those boats and, for the rest of his life, would insist he was the first person from the fleet to set foot in this world because he gave Lieutenant George Johnston a piggyback to land at Botany Bay. Presumably Lt Johnston thought *he* was first, because convicts didn't count.

By January 20, all the ships had arrived at Botany Bay. By this time, Phillip had pretty much decided the bay was a completely crap place to set up the penal colony; there was no supply of fresh water, the ground was swampy, the harbour wasn't big enough, or sheltered from the wind.

Phillip would have been pretty pissed off. "Jeez, they've sent me halfway around the world to this hole, where I'm supposed to set up a city that will one day have stupidly expensive property prices. Now I've got to go find some other place to put all these convicts. And maybe a place that also has a really cool spot where someone can build an opera house one day."

He'd come to a totally foreign place, in charge of loads of people, found the chosen destination was useless and now he had to scout around for somewhere else. Talk about a massive pain in the arse.

Luckily for him, there was a great spot just a short spurt up the coast. On the morning of January 21, he took a few of those longboats up the coast to check out a few places, one of which Captain Cook had mapped as he was sailing up the coast in 1770 but hadn't been buggered to hang a left and have a look.

Broken Bay was the first place they looked at and Phillip realized he'd hit the jackpot. And perhaps thought to himself Cook (well, actually it was the Endeavour's botanist Joseph Banks who had been the place's biggest fan) was an idiot for raving about the dump that was Botany Bay but ignoring this totes amazing place. For we know Broken Bay better as Sydney Harbour – a massive sheltered harbour with sections of coast deep enough that ships could park so close to the shore the sailors could tie them to trees on the shoreline. There was also a grand space for an opera house – and even a spiffy bridge not far at all from the spot Phillip chose to get this colony under way.

Meanwhile, soldiers and sailors were ashore back at Botany Bay. Some went exploring, others went fishing and others were hard at work digging holes for a sawpit. All the while they were watched and occasionally poked and prodded by the natives. One of their number scalded himself when, having never seen boiling water before, reached into some sailors' pot full of it to pull out a fish. There was often a friendly sense of curiosity from the Aboriginal people to the newcomers, largely because they'd expected these white guys would soon be newgoers too, just like all the other whities who had stopped by. If they'd known these strangers were going to hang around for hundreds of years, they mightn't have been so chilled.

On January 23, with James Squire and the other convicts still waiting to get the hell off those convict ships, Phillip returned from what is no w Port Jackson and told everyone they were moving to "the finest harbour in the world"; this place with a spring of water that he had chosen to call Sydney Cove.

The next day, with sailors and soldiers getting ready to leave, several French ships were spotted trying to enter Botany Bay. Bizarre, huh? The Brits went halfway around the world to a strange place and manage to bump into some Europeans after only a few days.

The English left the godforsaken piece of crap that was Botany Bay to the French and headed north on January 26. But as the First Fleet left, they gave the French a stunning display of British naval skill – the Friendship rammed the Prince of Wales, and then Squire's ship the Charlotte rammed the Friendship and almost came a cropper on the rocks.

The last ship in the fleet eventually made it to Sydney Cove at 7pm, by which time they'd missed the first Australia Day. Having gotten there at 3pm on January 26, the Supply disgorged its contents, including Governor Phillip and then hoisted the Union Jack, fired a few shots in the air and drank a toast. Then they all got Southern Cross tattoos and someone took down the flag and tied it around their neck like a cape.

Okay, maybe not those last bits.

8
Let's Talk About Sex
In which the convicts get off, some in more ways than one

On January 27, the unloading of the convicts began, and they went "thank God for that". Then they were put to work clearing land and they went "hang on, can we get back on the boat?". Squire himself likely had another day to wait before getting on dry land – the Charlotte's convict contingent wasn't disembarked until January 28 and, even though that was a Monday, there would be no long weekend for Australia Day.

Some convicts hated Sydney right from the start and tried to escape. Because escaping into the bush and trying to fend for yourself in a strange and isolated country is so much more sensible than staying in the camp where the food and shelter is. A few made their way south along native tracks to Botany Bay, where they begged the French to take them on board. The

French said whatever the French equivalent of "sucked in, you have to stay here and your descendants will one day be forced to pay ridiculous prices for a home" and sent them back to Sydney Cove. Except for one French-born convict conveniently named Peter Paris, who was secreted on board by sympathetic sailors. It wasn't a good choice for Paris, who would later be lost in the New Hebrides along with the rest of the French expedition.

The disembarkation of convicts was a gradual thing, which really sucked for the female convicts on the Lady Penrhyn. Having arrived in Botany Bay on January 20, they would have to wait a torturous two-and-a-half weeks to get off the boat. And when they finally set foot on the soil of what is now Circular Quay on February 6, they became participants in the first orgy in Australia.

Maybe.

The orgy on that thundery, wet night is much-beloved by historians desperate for something exciting to write about. But, if you ask me, the whole thing seems at least exaggerated or maybe even completely made up.

The sole piece of evidence for this is the diary of the Lady Penrhyn's doctor Arthur Bowes Smyth, who describes the women's disembarkation thusly; "The men got to them very soon after they landed and it is beyond my abilities to give a just description of the scene of debauchery and riot that ensued during the night."

Bowes Smyth was on the ship at the time of this observation. The ship wasn't near the shore – the women needed to be ferried to land in longboats – and it was dark and stormy. So he's seeing this "orgy" from a distance, at night and in the rain; all of which makes me at least a little bit skeptical as to the veracity of his account. Adding weight to this is the fact that no one else mentions this event in diaries or letters home. No one. Maybe it's just me, but if there had been a big rootfest that night on the shore of Sydney Cove, don't you think that a few other people might have noticed it? I certainly do.

While it is plausible that some women may have chosen to let loose after eight months at sea and nearly three weeks anchored offshore with land so close, a full-blown orgy would certainly have included more than a few rapes – not really the sort of thing historians should be going all "nudge-nudge, wink-wink" about.

The next day, Squire and all the other convicts were ordered to sit cross-legged on the ground like a bunch of schoolkids at an outdoor assembly. Then Governor Arthur Phillip, all done up in his fancy duds, read out the documents from the King that made him the boss of Sydney Cove. Reading accounts of the morning's event, it all seems quite dull and it's easy to imagine some of the convicts' attention wandering, or maybe they scratched their heads at some of the high-falutin' language coming from Phillip's mouth.

But there may have been one section that caught the attention of a convicted chicken thief like Squire. Bowes Smyth relates the morning in a very detailed diary entry. The part that Squire likely heard loud and clear was recorded by Bowes Smyth in his diary; "In England, thieving poultry was not punished by death; but here where a loss of that kind could not be supplied, it was of the utmost consequence to the settlement, as well as every other species of stock, as they were preserved for breeding. Therefore stealing the most trifling article of stock or provisions should be punished with death."

You stole a chook to get here, Squire. Do it again and you'll hang.

<u>9</u>

Hang Around

In which we find Arthur Phillip wasn't kidding about the whole "steal food and you're dead" thing

There was good reason for Arthur to make food-stealing punishable by death. The colony at Sydney Cove was a speck on the edge of a country that was at the arse-end of the world as far as England was concerned.

Every white person at Sydney Cove that day had a very clear understanding of how far away from home, help and supplies they were. They'd just spent eight months getting here; any ship carrying supplies would take a similar amount of time. Later, the colonists would find great farmland up the Parramatta River but, for the first few years from January 1788, it was going to be a precarious existence for convict and settler alike. In that open-air prison, food became the

No1 currency, so it made sense for Arthur to look to sentence to death anyone who tried to steal it.

To mete out punishments for stealing food and other crimes committed on Sydney Cove, a court was set up. It first sat on February 11 and the first case it heard was that of convict Sam Barsby who had gotten drunk and attacked two people with an adze – basically an axe.

Four days earlier, two seamen had stopped him and asked for directions to the women's camp – for exactly the reason you're thinking of. Barsby was obliging and was rewarded with a bottle of rum for his trouble; most of which he polished off soon thereafter.

He then staggered around a bit until he bumped into another convict and started arguing. Drum Major Cook told the pair to quit pissfarting about and get back to work. Barsby didn't take kindly to this and whacked Cook upside the head with his adze. Cook returned serve with his cane and two senior soldiers arrived and told Cook to take the drunk convict to jail. Another nearby marine, Drummer West, was called in to assist. So Barsby clobbered him too.

Eventually they got Barsby under control and he was taken to jail, where he was so abusive he was bound and gagged just to shut him up. In court, Barsby admitted the crimes but blamed it on the rum (well, derrr, Captain Obvious).

It did him no good – he was sentenced to 150 lashes and he'd be far from the last person to get whipped for drinking too much rum.

Two weeks later Arthur Phillip would have to put his money where his mouth was when it came to the theft of food. On February 27, four men, including young Thomas Barrett, who had already twice dodged the death sentence, stood accused of being in possession of food stolen for the storehouse.

Barrett and co-conspirators Henry Lovell, Joseph Hall and John Ryan were all found guilty. Barrett, Lovell and Hall were sentenced to swing at the end of a rope while Ryan was to receive 300 lashes.

That afternoon the convicts were ordered to a large Moreton Bay fig tree, located where The Rocks is now, so as to witness what happened when you stole food in the colony. The three condemned men arrived at the gallows, and, before they climbed the ladders under their nooses, a sentry arrived with a 24-hour stay for Lovell and Hall. This left Barrett to have his lights switched off alone.

"He expressed not the least sign of fear till he mounted the ladder," wrote Marine Lieutenant Ralph Clark in his diary, "and then he turned very pale and seemed very much shocked."

There was a delay in pulling the ladder out from under Barrett's feet. According to Clark, the hangman (a convict who had been dragooned into the role) had no stomach for the job and could only be coerced to do it under threat of being shot by the marines.

"Just before Barrett was turned off, he confessed the justice of his sentence, and that he had led a very wicked life," Clark wrote.

"He requested leave to speak to one of the convict men (a very bad kind of man) one Seddiway, which was granted him and he also expressed a wish to speak to one of the women convicts, but was refused. He then exhorted all of them to take warning by his unhappy fate and so launched into eternity. The body hung an hour and was then buried in a grave, dug very near the gallows."

The next afternoon Barrett's criminal cohorts Lovell and Hall made their second trip to that evil Moreton Bay fig as late summer rain tumbled from the sky. Prayers were offered for their souls and then a pardon arrived from Arthur Phillip; they wouldn't swing if they accepted a punishment of banishment to the "South Cape". Ryan was let off his 300 lashes too. Some months later, Phillip would say "hey, let's forget about that banishment thing. All is forgiven" and give all three complete pardons. Which must have had

Thomas Barrett turning over in his grave.

10
Been Caught Stealing

In which Squire pokes his head up for the first time since arriving in Sydney Cove

These days we like to think of James Squire as a big figure in the colony. After all, he's one of the few convicts most of us know by name, right? So he had to be a bit of a mover and shaker. Well, eventually he was; after he served his sentence, moved inland a bit to Kissing Point and conned others to sell him their land for pennies on the dollar.

But in the early years of the colony he wasn't that special. He was just another convict; albeit one who was a bit smarter than most. He seemed to realise the best course of action was to shut up and keep his head down.

Which would be why he appears nowhere in any official records or diaries throughout 1788. Whatever he was doing, he was doing it very quietly and making sure no one noticed. It's not until more than a year after the First Fleet's arrival, in March 1789, that Squire does something that draws attention to himself. And what he did was choose to stay up late one Sunday night.

At 10pm on March 1, Squire was still awake, sitting in his hut when he heard a rustling noise outside near the fence of his neighbour William Parr. He took a look outside to see what was going on and spotted a man darting out of the garden and over the hedge. A not-very-chivalrous man either, for he left behind two women, one of whom had a bag full of cabbages. The thieving pair had been caught red-handed. A convict himself, Squire could not arrest the pair, but he was forced to give evidence at their trial five days later on March 5.

The two women Squire saw that night were Tamasin Allen and Mary Turner, who had both sailed on the Lady Penrhyn. Allen seems to be the more devious of the two. Described as a "lustyish woman with black hair" at her trial in England, she was sentenced to seven years' transportation for assaulting and robbing a man who had just had his watch pilfered by someone else. Turner had the same seven-year sentence but her crime was to steal a few items of clothing amounting to little more than £2 from a house where no-one was home.

The pair were found guilty of stealing six cabbages from Parr's garden and sentenced to 50 lashes each – 25 immediately and the remainder to be administered on the next provision day. The women presumably escaped the death sentence for stealing food because they didn't pilfer it from the government stores. Or maybe the judge liked lusty women.

11
Smallpox Champion

In which the white man kills the native population without even trying. But they save one or two as well

It's quite likely that the first black man killed by the First Fleeters was actually one they brought with them. George Nelson, the cook on the convict ship Prince of Wales was "a negro", as described by First Fleet diarist Arthur Bowes Smyth (who doesn't even think enough of Nelson to bother mentioning him by name).

Things went very awry for Nelson on February 15, 1788, as he was getting off the Prince of Wales via a rope. "…two of the boys of that ship playing tricks with him", Bowes Smyth wrote, "shook him off the rope, and the poor fellow sunk down and was drowned, not being able to swim. Many sailors jumped overboard to save him, but he sunk and did not come up again."

Unlike Nelson's fate, early relations between the natives and the newcomers were relatively cordial, perhaps because the Aboriginal tribes figured this arrangement was temporary. The other times these weird-looking white guys turned up they hung around just long enough to get some food and water and then left.

So the natives apparently decided to treat them like less-than-welcome house guests – maybe if we give them what they want and humour them for a bit, they'll go away. But, after a while, it became clear to them that these interlopers weren't going away any time soon. Kind of like unwelcome house guests who start to pull out your sofa bed and ask if you have any bed sheets they could use.

That's when things started to get a bit testy on both sides. The locals start to have issues with the newbies taking all the fish, chopping down the trees and generally wrecking the joint and so some of them began poking various whities full of holes.

In turn the whities didn't like seeing their friends turned into human sieves and so decided to return serve. On March 6, 1789, sick of the natives' incursions into their camp, a posse of convicts downed tools and headed back along the track to Botany Bay to mete out some revenge.

According to Marine Watkin Tench's report, the Aboriginal tribe saw them coming a mile away and attacked.

"Our heroes (one wonders if Tench was taking the piss by calling them that) were immediately routed, and separately endeavoured to effect their escape by any means which were left. In their flight one was killed, and seven were wounded, for the most part very severely: those who had the good fortune to outstrip their comrades and arrive in camp, first gave the alarm; and a detachment of marines, under an officer, was ordered to march to their relief."

But they were too late to repel the attackers; though they did bring back the body of the dead convict. Phillip was incensed by the attack, as the convicts had fibbed to him and said they had been innocently picking sweet tea when they were suddenly set upon by the dastardly natives.

But his mood changed when some of the convicts finally told the truth; the next day the ringleaders all received 150 lashes. Phillip had Arabanoo – an Aboriginal man kidnapped in December 1788 in an odd effort by Phillip to improve relations – watch the convicts get whipped. Phillip felt it would be taken as a sign of his fairness in dealing with those who harmed

Aboriginal tribes. But, according to Tench, Arabanoo figured these white guys were sick in the head – "he displayed on the occasion symptoms of disgust and terror only".

Around the same time the colonists managed to kill off a number of Aboriginal people without even trying. In March and April, the settlers would routinely find bodies of native men, women and children in the inlets and coves of the harbour. The pustules all over their bodies were a clear indication they had died of smallpox.

"From the great number of dead natives found in every part of the harbour," wrote William Bradley, lieutenant on the Sirius, in early 1789, "it appears that the smallpox had made dreadful havock (sic) among them. We did not see a canoe or a native the whole way coming up the harbour and were told that scarce any had been seen lately, except laying dead in and about their miserable habitations, whence it appears that they are deserted by their companions as soon as the disorder comes out on them."

Smallpox was a disease well-known to the white settlers of Sydney Cove, as the scars some wore on their faces did attest.

But it was an entirely new – and extremely unwelcome – development for the Aboriginal people whose immune systems weren't really up to warding it off. And so they began dying. A number of suggestions for where the disease came from were floated. In a list of possibilities, Watkin Tench started off by blaming the French. Yep, it must have been those shifty cheese-eating surrender monkeys who had spent time in Botany Bay the previous year that had brought it with them.

He also made the faintly ridiculous suggestion that William Dampier introduced it when he landed in what is now Western Australia and it travelled all the way across the country to infect Aboriginal tribes on the east coast.

Bizarrely Tench places "hey maybe we brought it here 12 months ago" in last place on his list. Call me crazy, but if you set up camp in a location and, a year later, the native population starts karking it of a disease you're quite familiar with, then odds are pretty high that it's your fault.

In April, Phillip visited one of the beaches where bodies had been reported. There he found a boy aged nine or 10 pouring water on the head of an old man lying on the sand. Nearby was the body of a female child and her mother.

The old man and the boy were lifted into the boat and taken back to Sydney Cove, though not before

Arabanoo – who was on the boat, buried the female child.

The two survivors were taken to surgeon John White's hospital at Sydney Cove and put in quarantine. The boy's name was, apparently, Nanbaree – the word the old man called him. The man did not survive, but Nanbaree did. The surgeon White would adopt him, giving him a mouthful of a name in Andrew Sneap Hammond Douglass White.

Nanbaree would spend the rest of his life split between his native world and that of the newcomers. He would live in the settlement for a time and became a sailor. But when back in Sydney he would go bush and take part in a number of ritual battles. One such battle – his final one – would see him cross paths with James Squire.

12
Police and Thieves

*In which we find having convicts as police
isn't as unusual as it seems*

On the surface the story of James Squire spending
time as a police constable is strange. After all, he was
a convict, surely that's the sort of person who would
be last in line when you were choosing people to
enforce the law.

But, honestly, who else was going to do it? The First
Fleet was made up of convicts, marines and sailors.
The sailors weren't hanging around long after the
fleet's arrival, while the marines were resentful of the
very idea that they might serve as prison guards or
policemen. So the convicts were really the only choice.

It took everyone a little while to wake up to that fact
though. In a colony largely populated by criminals it
should come as no surprise that crime was a regular
occurrence ("hardly a night passing without the
commission of robbery", Tench wrote). By mid-1789

it had gotten so bad that even the convicts themselves had had enough and wanted something done.

In July of that year a convict named John Harris approached the powers that be with the idea of setting up a "Night Watch" with recruits coming from that pool of crims who could be trusted. On August 7, Phillip drew up the regulations for the Night Watch, which comprised 12 convicts split into four parties and who were fully authorised to patrol at all hours in the night.

Their remit was "to visit such places as may be deemed necessary for the discovery of any felony, trespass or misdemeanor and for the apprehending and securing for examination any person or persons that may appear to them concerned therein, either by entrance into any suspected hut or dwelling or by such other manner as may appear expedient."

The convicts were also authorised to apprehend any soldier or sailor who was "straggling about" after the drum signaling the start of the evening curfew had sounded. Funnily enough that didn't sit too well with the soldiers (the other convicts didn't take too kindly to the Night Watch either).

When a marine was found in the convict tents and detained by a member of the Night Watch, their commander (and total dickhead. Really, it's a historical fact) Major Robert Ross said his men would not "suffer themselves to be treated in that manner or to be controlled by the convicts". So Phillip backtracked and told the Night Watch to leave any soldier alone "unless he is found in a riot or committing any unlawful act".

In general the Night Watch was a success – in its early months crime did fall. By 1790, it started recruiting free settlers. But by 1799, its effect on crime was declining amid suggestions some officers were lazy or accepting bribes. And so, at the turn of the century, the Night Watch system was scrapped and replaced with the model that would soon see James Squire as a member of the constabulary.

<u>13</u>
Whip It

In which we look at the truth behind what happened the second time James Squire and the law crossed paths

On a warm spring day in November 1789, the event that would become the most well-known tale in the life of James Squire took place. But before we go any further, we need to go back eight months, to another event occurred that showed how seriously Arthur Phillip took the theft of supplies and also makes you wonder if Squire may have gotten off a bit lightly.

On March 18 a marine dawn patrol found a broken key in the lock of the door where the government stores were housed. Looking inside they found a cask had been opened and some provisions removed. Eager for a lead, marine John Easty took the lock and broken key to the convict blacksmith to see if he recognised it.

According to Easty, the blacksmith "immediately knew them to belong to a Private Joseph Hunt, the same who in the course of the preceding month received seven hundred lashes [for being absent from his post in February] and who had some time back brought the key to this blacksmith to be altered".

When approached to explain himself, Hunt rolled over in about 10 seconds – on the condition he would be pardoned. And did he have a story to tell.

For it wasn't just Hunt who was involved in the theft of food, nor was this a one-time thing. Hunt dobbed in six other marines – Richard Dukes, James Baker, James Brown, Thomas Jones, Richard Asky and Luke Haynes – as members of a gang that had been ripping off the government stores for at least three weeks.

The gang's spree began under a vow of secrecy, with the threat of death at the hands of the others should any one of them blab to the law. They acquired several keys from other convicts and settlers and then had the blacksmith reshape them (there being no Mr Minit in Sydney Cove in 1789) so they fit each of the three different locks on the government stores.

On nights when one of the seven was posted as a sentinel at the storehouse, two other members would turn up with a key and grab whatever they could carry.

"If the patrols visited the store while they chanced to be within its walls," wrote judge advocate David Collins just after the ring was broken up, "the door was found to be locked and secure, the sentinel alert and vigilant on his post and the store apparently safe".

It only went pear-shaped when one of the conspirators got stupid and greedy. The unnamed member decided to have a go at swiping something on his own, without another gang member on guard.

While standing at the door having just opened the lock with the key, he heard the patrol approaching. Realising the patrol would check the lock, he went to re-lock it and remove the key. But in a panic to avoid being discovered, he turned the key the wrong way and then could not remove it. So he was forced to snap it off, leaving part of it still in the lock for the patrol to find.

Some of the gang members confessed before their trial. In his confession Haynes included a list of some of the stolen items – 100 gallons of liquor (old rum, Rio rum and wine) 500 weight of flour, 16 pounds of butter, a bag of bread and eight pounds of leaf tobacco.

The trial of the marines was held on the afternoon of March 26. In an ominous sign, the gallows were erected before the trial had even finished. At 2.30 that afternoon, all six marines received a death sentence while Hunt was pardoned. That didn't sit well with the condemned men, who all protested from the scaffold that Hunt was the one who orchestrated the whole damn thing.

The marines who watched the hanging weren't happy to see the court and – by extension – Governor Phillip sentence six of their comrades to death. For a time now, when it came to punishment, rations and other areas, the marines felt they were being treated the same or worse than the convicts. And of course, the men in the red coats saw themselves as quite a bit higher up society's ladder than the convicts.

It was part of Phillip's plan to treat everyone as equally as possible, for he saw this as the best way to give the colony a good chance to grow. The hanging of six marines couldn't have been easy, but it also sent two strong messages out to everyone in this little speck on the east coast of Australia – he was serious about killing anyone who stole food from the government, and it didn't matter who you were.

That's something to keep in mind as we look at the events on a Saturday in mid-November, where James Squire gets punished for stealing from the government. Something else worth considering is that what you've heard about the day Squire was whipped across his bare back is probably not true. Which is a pity, given that, thanks to the Squire mythology, this day has come to be seen as the central moment in his life.

The popular telling has it that Squire got caught stealing a herb called horehound to make beer (some versions claim he also stole paper to use as labels on the bottles). He mounted the defence that it was for, variously, a sick friend or his pregnant girlfriend but was still found guilty. His sentence was 300 lashes, 150 immediately and the rest when he could bear it. Though he never got that second lot of lashes.

Okay, let's start unpicking this. Yes, Squire was caught for stealing, was found guilty and sentenced to 300 lashes. Beyond that, much of this tale is just not backed up by any actual evidence.

Looking at the notes of Squire's trial one thing is immediately apparent – there is no mention that he stole horehound. The only stolen item mentioned by name is pepper – which is sometimes misrepresented as "paper" in the Squire mythology.

The court records for that day (written by someone with appalling penmanship, may I add) state that our man was charged with "feloniously stealing a certain quantity of medicines being hospital stores, the property of the crown, and one pound of pepper, the property of Mr White and others". That's it – no horehound mentioned at all.

The idea that he'd stolen horehound is a later addition to the tale, apparently to bolster the idea that he was stealing the ingredients to make beer. Perhaps its origin comes from a 1916 article written by Walter Hibble for the *Journal of the Royal Australian Historical Society*. As quoted in a later *Journal* article by David Hughes (called 'Australia's First Brewer'), Hibble wrote "It is said that horehound beer, or what was called beer, was made in the early days from the honey of the small Australian bee, bittered with this herb." As a frustrated Hughes points out, Hibble offers no source for this claim.

The bigger issue here, though, is the idea that Squire was stealing beer ingredients. It's a cool story to stick on your beer bottle labels, but the court records simply don't support it. In fact, they make it impossible. If he's planning to make beer with these stolen items, why was Squire planning to send them to Norfolk Island?

Yep, that's where they were going, according to evidence given before the court by John Frederick, a seaman on the Norfolk Island-bound Supply. Frederick said Squire and an unnamed female convict approached him around two weeks before the trial to ask if he could to take a bag and a bedstead on board for a female convict, to be delivered to her when the ship arrived at Norfolk Island.

A day or so later, Squire handed Frederick the bag and the seaman – being a nosy bugger – looked inside. According to the trial notes, "when opened [it] was found to contain the articles the prisoner stands charged with stealing". I think you'd agree it's pretty hard to brew beer with ingredients you're sending away on a ship.

So, the idea he was swiping the ingredients with which to brew beer is rubbish. Instead, let's look at the suggestion that Squire's theft was to aid his pregnant girlfriend. At the time he was sprung, Squire was seeing the convict Mary Spencer. She would give birth to Squire's son Francis on August 1, 1790. If you do the maths, that means Francis would have been conceived a few weeks before Squire's theft. Which makes the "pregnant girlfriend" claim a little more feasible.

Now here's where things get interesting. Spencer gave birth to Francis on Norfolk Island, where she had been since December 1789. And the ship that took her there? None other than Frederick's HMS Supply. And when did it leave? November 11, just days before Squire's trial and a week after Squire's chat with

Frederick.

That much is fact, but let me now float a theory. When Frederick said Squire spoke to him, the man was accompanied by an unnamed female convict, the very same convict on whose behalf Squire was asking for the items to be taken with her to Norfolk Island.

It hardly seems a giant leap to suggest that unnamed woman was the newly pregnant Spencer, who was shortly to leave for Norfolk Island on Frederick's ship. Nor does it seem a leap to suggest that whatever items Squire stole were indeed to provide comfort to his pregnant girlfriend while on a rock out in the middle of the ocean.

Sure, this is circumstantial evidence, but jeez, it is compelling. Certainly more so than the idea he was stealing the ingredients for beer. Which really casts a huge amount of doubt on the back story behind that One-Fifty Lashes beer put out under the James Squire brand.

To go a bit further, there is also doubt on that beer's name itself. The records state Squire's punishment was to receive 150 lashes now and the remainder at a later date. So he gets the first 150 lashes and then, so the myth goes, that's all he got because he was brewing beer for high-ranking marines and they got him out of the second half of his sentence.

I doubt that very much. The marines saw six of their fellow soldiers hang for theft six months earlier, and they're going to let a lowly convict skip out on sentence? That's pretty hard to swallow.

The basis of this claim is that there is no record of Squire getting those second 150 lashes. There are two things worth pointing out here. Firstly, the idea of splitting floggings up like that was not at all uncommon. We just saw an example of it a few chapters ago with cabbage thieves Tamasin Allen and Mary Turner – who got a sentence of 50 lashes split into two lots of 25.

Flogging was a painful punishment but dish out too much in one go and you could kill the person. On top of that, splitting it up would have created the mental punishment of knowing you're only halfway through, that you've got another bout of whipping in a week or so.

Secondly, the absence of evidence that Squire didn't get lashes 151-300 can't be taken as proof that he dodged them. I'd actually argue that it means he *did* get them. Look at it this way; the court hands down a sentence and expects it to be carried out. The only reason there would be any further record made was if the sentence was commuted, or if the course of the law changed direction in some other way. That there was no further record suggests to me there was no change in the law's direction and that Squire got all 300 lashes.

As to why he was lashed for stealing from the government while six marines were hanged for the same offence, well that likely has something to do with what they stole. Unlike the marines, Squire wasn't stealing food but rather hospital supplies. Still something to be punished for but not putting the fledgling colony at risk like stealing food.

For the rest of his life he would carry the scars of that day on his back. Scars which represented the price of love, of trying taking care of your pregnant girlfriend and future child. You ask me, that's a far better story than trying to suggest he was stealing stuff to make beer.

14

The Dead Heart

In which Governor Phillip decides kidnapping is a great way to improve race relations

As white guys go, Arthur Phillip was a fair man when it came to dealing with the native population. Other white guys may have set about eradicating them just to get the blighters out of the way. Because, after all, all dark-skinned people were savages unlikely to ever evolve to the level of white people, am I right? Yes, of course I'm being sarcastic.

But not Phillip. He could have ordered the military to knock them off, but he didn't. Not even when they chose to kill some white guys. Well, not for a whole two years, anyway.

However, the governor did have some curious ideas

about dealing with the natives. One of which was his belief that kidnapping Aboriginal men was a great idea that would bring the two races closer. His thinking was that the kidnapped men would serve as an intermediary/hostage between the interlopers and the natives. Phillip outlined his plan in a letter to Lord Sydney back home in England.

"It was absolutely necessary that we should attain their language, or teach them ours, that the means of redress might be pointed out to them, if they are injured, and to reconcile them by showing the many advantages they would enjoy by mixing with us."

Advantages like being kidnapped and held against your will, perhaps. Phillip was so enamored of this idea of kidnapping that he did it twice.

On December 30, 1788, Phillip ordered two boats to head down the harbour with orders to seize some natives. They arrived at Manly Cove and found several native men standing on the water's edge. The English coaxed them to their boats and, when the natives got close enough, the visitors pounced. They grabbed two of the men and looked to shove them in the boat.

One managed to escape by dragging the sailor holding onto him into deeper water until he let go while the other was thrown in the boat, a manacle quickly placed around his ankle and he was put under the eye of a trusty convict.

With that, the kidnappers made their getaway "and an attack from the shore instantly commenced," wrote Watkin Tench, "they threw spears, stones, firebrands and whatever else presented itself at the boats". But to no avail – their companion had been snatched away.

After some understandable crying and wailing, the captive "sullenly submitted to his destiny". In the early days of his captivity he was introduced to the weird ways of the west – including multi-storey buildings (apparently he thought the people he saw hanging out of the first floor of buildings were standing on someone else's shoulders). But he refused to tell them his name – so they called him Manly, after the cove from which he was swiped.

In time he was twice taken back to Manly Cove to show the rest of his tribe that he was alright and perhaps tell them how tops the English were. On the second visit, no one showed up on the beach – likely because they feared it was a trap and the white ghosts would snap them up too. After this visit, when it must have seemed to him that his tribe had cast him aside, he revealed his real name was Arabanoo.

He never did learn English well enough to act as a conduit between the British and the Aboriginal population which, you'll remember, was the whole point of the kidnapping. After five months in the colony, Arabanoo would fall victim to the smallpox that was ravaging the Aboriginal population in the vicinity of Sydney Cove. He passed away on May 18, 1789, and Phillip had him buried in his garden. And then waited a whole six months before he decided to kidnap some more natives.

On November 25, 11 days after Squire was sentenced to 300 lashes, Lieutenant William Bradley was ordered to head back to that happy hunting ground of Manly Cove to nab some more locals. Using some fish, they lured several men away from a larger group and, when Bradley gave the signal, the men in the ship grabbed two of them and took them away.

To his credit Bradley found this whole kidnapping thing quite ugly – "it was by far the most unpleasant service I was ever ordered to execute," he wrote in his journal, after describing the disturbing scene at Manly Cove.

"The noise of the men, crying and screaming, of the women and children together with the situation of the two miserable wretches in our possession was really a most distressing scene; they were much terrified, one of them particularly so. The other frequently called out to those onshore apparently very much enraged with them."

Once back at Sydney Cove, there was no need for the pair to hide their names; Nanbaree, the young boy found suffering from smallpox on the beach earlier that year, instantly recognised the pair as Colbee and Bennelong.

The pair were washed, shorn and each had an iron shackle attached to their ankles with a convict told to watch them lest they try and escape. Which was exactly what Colbee had in mind. Showing he was, as Captain Hunter wrote, "very far from being destitute of observation and cunning", Colbee lulled his captors into thinking he was comfortable within the colony.

One night he was sitting just outside the door of their house, with his convict overseer inside eating dinner while holding the rope that was attached to Colbee's shackle. Colbee pulled the rope from the shackle and then jumped the backyard fence and walked away. According to Lieutenant Bradley, Bennelong was also close to freeing the rope from his shackle and following Colbee when the latter's escape was detected.

So Bennelong missed his chance and would bide his time in the colony, becoming friends with the governor and learning about the English before his shackle was removed in April 1790. Early on the morning of May 3, he pretended to be sick and was taken downstairs to the backyard to take care of business. In this case "business" being jumping over the back fence and walking off. Years later he, like Nanbaree, would walk into James Squire's life.

15
Sweet Child O' Mine

*In which a marine tries to swap his hat for
an Aboriginal child*

By February 1790 Squire was a servant for marine lieutenant and president of the I Hate Female Convicts club Ralph Clark. That month he found himself accompanying Clark on several exploratory trips to Lane Cove, with a view to interacting with the locals. And, like Arthur Phillip, trying to get his hands on one.

On February 14, Clark met two natives and gave them a hatchet in exchange for two spears. The following day Clark, Squire and his other convict servant (who we only seem to know by his surname of Davis) headed back up river looking for those two native men. Nearing the spot where they met the previous day, Clark could see no one on the beach. He called out for them and they responded and so he made to get out of his boat, much to the concern of the fearful Davis, who Clark described in his journal as "one of the greatest cowards living".

In a move that suggests Clark placed a good deal of trust in Squire (perhaps because of his time in the military back in 1774) the marine gave him a gun. "Before I left the boat I desired Ellis [another servant on the trip] and Squires ... that should [they] attempt to throw any of their spears at me or them, to fire without waiting for my orders," Clark wrote in his journal.

But the Aboriginal men were unarmed and so no bullets were fired. Clark then made his servants join him onshore – "Davis trembled the whole time" – and as he could hear crying children, asked to see them. He handed the children small pieces of coloured cloth and then put forward a rather one-sided deal.

"I asked them if they would give me the children for my hat which they seemed to wish most for, but they would not on any account part with their children, which I liked them for."

Clark makes no mention of what the native men thought of him for trying to buy their children with a frigging hat. In his diary he brags about how he could have easily kidnapped the men but chose not to because it would be "very ungenerous" of him after they had placed such trust in him. But trying to buy someone's kids with a hat was perfectly fine.

The next morning, a Sunday, Clark dragged Squire and Davis out to Lane Cove again. He found no sign of the pair whose children he tried to buy the day before but he did spot another Aboriginal man armed with two spears, who took off as soon as he realised Clark was coming ashore.

Apparently decided that chasing after someone while armed with a gun is not at all a threatening gesture, Clark armed himself, told Squire and Davis to do likewise, and then hared off into the bush to look for the man (and perhaps ask if he had any children he wanted to sell). They found no sign of the man but, on the way back to their boat, did find something else – a human skeleton.

It still had some hair and skin attached to the skull, which Clark saw was light brown in colour and therefore could not be an Aboriginal skeleton. So Clark concluded that it "must belong to some unfortunate person that was killed by the natives or, what is much more dreadful than being killed by the natives, that of losing one self and perishing with hunger."

Clark took the skull back to the settlement, believing the skeleton to be that of sailor Francis Hill who had gone missing in November 1789 when walking in the bush towards Sydney Cove. After surgeons examined it they concluded it was instead the skull of a convict who had gone missing a year ago. Several days later, Clark returned to Lane Cove with the skull and buried it along with the rest of the skeleton.

These Lane Cove exploits are interesting for what they hint at about Squire. It is hard to imagine a marine lieutenant giving a weapon to any old convict and expecting him to act as a bodyguard of sorts. Especially not when, as it appears from Clark's description of events, he would have had his back to Squire at least some of the time. He surely had to have faith in Squire's character, that he would not aim up and simply shoot him in the back.

It shows that, in the government's eye, Squire may have been in the upper ranks of the convicts. It also lends a small amount of plausibility to a particularly questionable claim regarding the life of James Squire – that he was a bodyguard to Governor Phillip. Both online and in print there is a quote suggesting he protected Phillip, who "felt safer with Squire than with the marines". There is never a source given for this quote, which in and of itself makes its veracity a little suss if you ask me. Also, I couldn't find this quote in any document of the time – nor could I find a single mention of Squire being a bodyguard of the governor. The governor himself certainly never mentioned him in his own journal – a curious omission if he did hold Squire in such high regard.

The "bodyguard" theory has it that Squire was present in that capacity on Manly Cove on a Tuesday afternoon in early September 1790 when Phillip visited the escaped native Bennelong and got speared through the shoulder. If Squire was there, then he was a bit crap as a bodyguard because he let his boss get skewered.

But here's the thing. There are a number of written accounts of that day, where an associate of Bennelong speared the governor in his presence (in what now seems a clear case of payback for his kidnapping) but not a single one of then mentions Squire. Marine Captain David Collins, Marine Lieutenant Henry Waterhouse and Phillip himself were all on the beach that day and all of them left behind a written account of the spearing. None of them mention Squire; in fact it's only Collins and Waterhouse – both armed with muskets – who accompanied Phillip along the beach to his rendezvous with a spear. And the governor asked for both of them to come with him onto the sand.

Now, you have to ask yourself, if Phillip saw Squire as such a trusted bodyguard, more trusted than the marines even, then why is it them and not Squire the governor turned to for protection on the afternoon of September 7?

To me, the most likely answer is because Squire wasn't there and he wasn't Phillip's bodyguard either.

16
Gimme Head

In which we discover Arthur Phillip's surprising interest in severed Aboriginal heads, which gives him a few degrees of separation to Adolf Hitler and the Nazis

This chapter really has nothing to do with Squire at all and, strictly speaking, probably shouldn't appear in a biography of the man. But, honestly, it's just too good a story to pass up – the fact that Governor Phillip had a thing for Aboriginal heads. Though only if they were separated from their bodies.

Sir Joseph Banks was dead keen to get his hands on some native skulls and Arthur Phillip was only too happy to oblige. A letter from Phillip to Banks in July 1790 includes the rather ominous sentence "I shall send skulls by the [HMS] Gorgon". It's shocking today how casual Phillip seems about sending the head of a deceased human being over to England – it's almost as though he didn't think they were as important as white folk.

In December of that year, Phillip comes up with a way to get a great big sack full of Aboriginal heads. It started on December 3, when Phillip's gamekeeper, John McIntyre, was speared by an Aboriginal man while on a hunting expedition to Botany Bay. It wasn't exactly out of the blue – Watkin Tench reckoned the gamekeeper had killed a few natives in his time and the marine had noted how those Aboriginals who hung around Sydney Cove had a real hatred of him.

The spear passed between two of McIntyre's ribs and pierced his lung. With the spear sticking out of him McIntyre made it back to Sydney Cove but died three days later. The man who did the spearing was Pemulwuy, a real arse-kicking Aborigine. If he was a white guy they would have made an action film about him by now. Guaranteed. Unlike a number of his countrymen, Pemulwuy wanted nothing to do with the whitefellas and the spearing of McIntyre marked the start of a 12-year guerilla war against them. He would lead others on raids of settlers' farms, where crops were burnt and livestock killed. The warrior became a fearful figure in the minds of the white settlers, a man who seemingly could not be killed – despite almost making a jingling sound when he walked because of all the pieces of bullets in him.

During an attack on farms at Toongabbie in 1797, he was repeatedly shot at and ended up with seven pieces of buckshot in his head and body. The settlers took him to hospital, put him in ankle irons and went "woo-hooh! We got him!". And then the guy - full of shrapnel and in irons – managed to escape. "Holy shit," the settlers said, "he's going to be REALLY mad now". On the other hand, the Aborigines said, "dude, you're so awesome!". But they didn't say it in English, obviously. He went on fighting whitey for five more years, until he finally found out he wasn't impervious to bullets when he was shot and killed in 1802.

But let's go back to that spearing of McIntyre that started the whole thing. By now, Phillip had had it up to here with Aborigines killing white people – it wasn't like the English had taken the *whole* country anyway, he thought, why can't they go live somewhere else? So he cracked it big time and called for Tench. And a big hessian sack.

He wanted the former to go hunting for Aborigines and make sure he killed at least 10 of them. And the sack was to put their heads in and bring them back to Phillip. But Arthur wasn't a savage; Tench was to only kill men, women and children were to be left untouched.

He asked Tench what he thought, and Tench basically said "how about, instead of killing 10 of them, we just kidnap six of them". Despite the fact this meant he wouldn't get 10 skulls, Phillip was okay with this and Tench recorded the governor's response in his journal – "if six cannot be taken, let this number be shot. Should you, however, find it practicable to take so many, I will hang two, and send the rest to Norfolk Island for a certain period, which will cause their countrymen to believe we have dispatched them secretly."

Ahh, the English thought they were so clever. But, despite hunting with two lieutenants and 46 marines, Tench didn't even catch single native let alone six in what was a three-day expedition. After returning empty-handed Phillip sent Tench out again and the soldier had the apparently genius idea to walk through the bush at night so as to surprise the natives. But that was rather unsuccessful, and led to both he and the majority of the marines getting stuck in the mud of Wolli Creek and wrecking their muskets. They freed themselves, rested on the banks of the creek for a few hours, then said "bugger this" and headed back to Sydney Cove.

Phillip eventually did get his hands on a skull – we don't know whose – and sent it over to Banks (who would also get Pemulwuy's head in a jar of spirits when he was shot and killed in 1802. It's now believed to be somewhere in the British Museum of Natural History but no one's been able to find it and send it home).

According to Tom Keneally in *Commonwealth of Thieves*, Banks sent the mystery skull to a Professor Johann Friedrich Blumenbach of the University of Gottingen. The professor believed that Caucasians "were the founding form of the human group, while other races had degenerated from this primary type because of climatic variations". In time, Blumenbach's work – based partially on skulls acquired from dead Aborigines at Sydney Cove – would be grasped with both hands by the Nazis as proof of Aryan supremacy.

So nice work, Arthur Phillip.

17

I Fought the Law

*In which we discover yet another time
Squire was in trouble with the law*

When it comes to Squire being on the wrong side of the law in Sydney Cove, people tend to think it only happened once – that time where he got lashed for stealing the ingredients to make beer (even though we now know that beer-making story is rubbish).

But Squire didn't go on the straight and narrow after those 300 lashes no doubt removed a lot of skin off his back and left a scar or two. He had another go at breaking the law almost two years later – though we only know about this instance because he got caught.

Who's to say he didn't break the law several other times in the intervening two years but managed to get away with it? After all, the records of the settlement of Sydney only record those not smart enough to evade detection; by definition, the names of those clever buggers who flew below the radar and never got nabbed by the Sydney Cove fuzz are unknown to us.

Squire's second brush with the law saw him front up to the court on Friday, August 19, 1791, "charged with buying the necessaries of Francis MacKewen, private soldier in the New South Wales Corp", according to the trial transcript. In this instance "necessaries" were clothes; specifically a pair of shirts.

They weren't both for Squire; he was going halfsies with his accomplice, a fellow convict by the name of John Cross, who had been sent to Sydney for stealing a sheep. The English took sheep theft very seriously – Cross had been sentenced to death before it was commuted to seven years' transportation on the First Fleet ship Alexander.

In the early years of the colony it was teetering on the brink of starvation from time to time. The crops hadn't grown as well as expected and much of the livestock wandered off into the bush not long after landing ("Hey dude, where's my cow?"). It led to the governor having to cut the rations several times and to eyes looking out to sea in the hope they would spot the sails of a supply ship. Which is why Private MacKewen sold his shirts; his stomach was growling and items of clothing aren't renowned for satisfying hunger. The rice and meat Squire and Cross gave him in exchange for the shirts, however, that would quieten his tummy rumbles quite nicely.

According to the trial transcript, none of the participants felt they were breaking the law. "The prisoners say they did not know they were doing anything wrong. The soldier said he was starving and assured them they could not be brought into trouble," the transcript read.

But into trouble they could indeed be brought; for their haberdashery crimes Squire and Cross each had to pay a fine of £5, due in three weeks' time. And no doubt Squire's back was relieved it wouldn't cop another lashing.

The fine, which was quite a lot of money in that time, has been used by some as proof that Squire's brewing – which seems to have started a year earlier on a small scale – had very quickly become a money spinner. The thinking here is that the court would only impose such a large fine if they knew Squire had the wherewithal to pay it. This, like the "One-Fifty Lashes" tale, is an example of the skewed thinking that surrounds James Squire's story.

Today, we know him mainly as the country's first brewer, so when we look back at his life, anything he does is affected by that knowledge. The claim of "oh, he was making beer" becomes an explanation for various things that happened in his life – even if there is no evidence to support it.

In the case of his being fined £5 because he was flush with cash from brewing on the side – well, that's absolute crap. To prove this, we only need to go back three weeks, to July 25, 1791, and the case of William Bond. Guess was he was pinged for? Yep, buying the necessaries of a marine. Bond bought some pants from Private John Kennedy for three and a half pounds of rice. His punishment? A fine of £5.

Further to this, judge advocate David Collins wrote a comment on Bond's trial.

"A practice having been discovered, of purchasing the soldiers regimental necessaries for the purpose of disposing of them among the shipping, and this requiring a punishment that should effectually check it, Bond, a convict who baked for the hospital and others, was brought before two magistrates, and being convicted of having bought several articles of wearing apparel which had been served to a soldier, was sentenced to pay the penalty prescribed by an act of parliament, £5, or on failure, within a certain time, to go to prison."

Ergo, Squire wasn't fined a fiver because he was stinking rich from brewing. He was fined £5 because the powers that be wanted to stamp out the practice of soldiers selling off their uniforms. And he was the first person caught buying them after Collins made that note. So he was made an example of, so others got the message. Perhaps they did – it doesn't appear that anyone else got caught buying soldiers' uniforms that year.

18
No Word From China

In which we take another slight diversion to tell a story that has nothing to do with Squire, but is a great story nonetheless

Some convicts who were disgorged from boats onto the soil of Sydney Cove figured they were stuck there. But some looked off into the distance and were heartened by what they didn't see – fences or walls. If a convict was daring (or perhaps stupid) enough they could just walk off and escape.

Some tried this and never returned; a fact some foolish people took to mean they had found freedom when, more likely, they had found death through either starvation or angry natives.

Irish convicts who arrived in Sydney got it into their heads that China lay somewhere on the other side of the bush that ringed the colony. Walk far enough and you'd find freedom in another country. It was a rationale seemingly borne of the perverse logic that both Sydney and China were so distant from England that they must surely sit in close proximity to each other. So various groups of Irish set out – some rumoured to be armed with a compass drawn onto a piece of paper – to find an Asian promised land.

The first group to give it a go was made up of 20 male convicts and a pregnant female. On November 1, 1791, they took tomahawks, knives and a week's food and walked off into the bush surrounding Parramatta. These people, who would gain the somewhat mocking name of "Chinese Travellers", were not at all successful in discovering China. The pregnant woman was the first to be found just a few days later, having been separated from the group soon after leaving. Others were captured to the north, "in a state of deplorable wretchedness, naked, and nearly worn out with hunger", wrote David Collins.

Governor Phillip slapped his forehead at their stupidity. He then rounded up all the convicts and read them the riot act – anyone who did this dumb "escape to China" thing again would be hunted by soldiers with orders to shoot on sight. Those who were returned would be dumped on an island in the middle of the harbour, or chained together and fed bread and water for the remaining term of their sentence. But it didn't work, for others would try their hand. Not even the ridicule those early escapees copped was enough to make them change their mind.

Some of those first 21 Chinese Travellers quickly looked to change their story once they saw what Watkin Tench described as "the merriment excited at their expense" when the populace found out why they escaped. The remainder made out that "their reason for running away was on account of being overworked and harshly treated, and that they preferred a solitary and precarious existence in the woods to a return to the misery they were compelled to undergo".

But Tench visited the survivors of the 21 in hospital shortly before returning to England and found that, yes, they *were* looking for China.

"They answered that they were certainly made to believe (they knew not how) that at a considerable distance to the northward existed a large river, which separated this country from the back part of China; and that when it should be crossed (which was practicable) they would find themselves among a copper-coloured people, who would receive and treat them kindly."

<u>19</u>

The Imposter

In which we wonder, just who the hell is Phillip Morris?

After his first Sydney Cove love Mary Spencer left for Norfolk Island in November 1789 with what would be Squire's fourth child (counting the other three forever left behind in London) in her belly, Squire didn't immediately shack up with the first female that walked past.

Though, at the same time, he didn't plan to wait for her to come back either. Nor did he appear to show any strong interest in his son, Francis, who was born on Norfolk Island on August 1 1790, preferring to make him her responsibility. Until he died, it seems the last thing he did for her and Francis was steal those hospital stores.

Mary would return to Sydney in 1796, having already hooked up with NSW Marine private John

Palmer (perhaps she figured Squire wouldn't be waiting around for her). By this time, Squire was well and truly onto his next relationship, one that would create a further six children.

His new love interest was Elizabeth Mason, a convict on the Mary Ann, which formed part of the Third Fleet. Busted for stealing quite an array of items including a table cloth, two linen sheets, two waistcoats, a silver spoon, eight pillow cases and a whole lot of handkerchiefs, Elizabeth ended up in Sydney on July 9, 1791. As well as Elizabeth, the Mary Ann carried something else that would come to mean a lot to Squire – instructions to the governor that time-expired convicts were to be granted a parcel of land. In the coming years Squire would use that rule to amass quite a sizeable estate.

The presence of a Third Fleet might surprise those who presumed there was only one lot of convicts – the First Fleet – brought to Australia. In fact, the British kept fobbing their criminals off on Australia for ages. The last convict transport disgorged its contents on the shores of Western Australia in 1868 – 80 years after the colony of Sydney Cove was founded.

Mason's voyage on the Third Fleet was far better than the mess that was the Second Fleet. Run by slave traders Camden, Calvert and King, they were paid by the government based on the number of convicts embarked, not landed. Which, of course, meant the slavers had no financial incentive or interest in keeping their charges alive.

And so they didn't. More than 100 prisoners died in the fleet and almost 500 were landed sick. Some of the dead were simply flung over the sides of the ships in the harbour and left to float ashore. If that didn't mark the slavers down as total scumbags, they went on to sell the leftover provisions on board to the starving settlers of Sydney Cove at huge mark-ups.

So Elizabeth walks ashore at Sydney Cove in July and it seems is almost immediately chatted up by Squire. She would give birth in May of the following year – so by doing the nine-month math – Mason and Squire lay with each other some time in September 1791. Which meant Squire didn't waste any time.

Their first-born child would create a small mystery that remains unsolved to this day. Priscilla was born on May 29, 1792. But the records of the christening state the father to be Phillip Morris, even though there is no record of anyone by that name living in Sydney Cove. In Squire's will, he claims Priscilla as his, calling her "a natural born daughter of mine by the said Elizabeth Mason". Which leads one to wonder why he chose to use the name "Phillip Morris" when recording the christening.

The reason for this we can only guess at. Was Squire trying to hide his relationship with Mason from someone, perhaps Mary Spencer? Was it a protest vote of sorts because he had doubts that he really was Priscilla's father? Did the priest just make a very, very bad typo?

Or was it an effort to leave Squire some wiggle room to avoid a law put in place in April of the previous year that would make it hard for him to return home to England if he so chose? The governor had decreed that time-expired convicts could not depart the colony and leave wives or children behind "until they had found sufficient security for such wives or children as long as they might remain after them," judge advocate David Collins recorded. Basically, the husband had to make sure they'd be okay without him around, financially speaking.

Priscilla was the first child Squire had fathered since the law had been passed. With his seven-year sentence due to end in a little over two years, Squire no doubt had one eye on the time he would become a free man. Was he thinking about heading back home to London when he got his freedom in 1795? If so, then maybe the Phillip Morris alias was a clumsy way for him to avoid having to provide for Elizabeth and Priscilla. If he did choose to leave, he could point to the document that listed Phillip Morris as the father, say "not my responsibility", jump on the next boat and head home.

That may not have been his motivation at all. But the move to hide the paternity of Priscilla does hint at some at least slightly sinister motive, don't you think?

<u>20</u>
Sign Your Name

In which James Squire gets invited to a
wedding

On June 13, 1793, convicts Matthew Gibbons and Margaret Gordon got hitched. Not much is known about the bride, but the groom came over on the Second Fleet (on the Surprize, the ship that brought Squire brewing rival John Boston to town. We'll hear more about him in the next chapter). Gibbons was done for stealing one-and-a-quarter pounds of tea and got seven years in Sydney for his trouble.

In Sydney Cove he ran a pub (which was more like a room with a few containers of beer than anything we might call a pub today) named The Dragoon in George Street. In the same year he was married, Gibbons joined the NSW Corps. According to Michael Flynn's book *The Second Fleet*, he headed back to England with the disgraced corps when they left. He and Margaret had two children in England before heading back to Sydney for 13 years, then went back to the Mother Country and then back to Sydney again, where he would ultimately kark it as an old man.

But what is relevant to us is that James Squire was a witness to that couple's special day. And it's special for us because he signed his name on the marriage certificate. Near as I can find, that's the only thing we have written in his own hand (though I'm pretty sure he did initialise his own will). Which makes it pretty important if you're a massive James Squire geek.

What's also worthwhile about the signature is that he was able to write it at all. This means he was literate – he could spell and write his own name, which shows he had some level of education. Some on the First Fleet couldn't write and would initial any documents with an X. The bride Margaret Gordon was one of them – instead of a signature, she scrawled an X next to where someone else has written her name.

Secondly, it's worth noting that, in his signature, James Squire drops the S at the end of his name. From before the time of the First Fleet through to his death notice in the *Sydney Gazette*, his name is consistently written as Squires. And yet when the man writes his own name, he spells it without the S. Weird. Even weirder is his gravestone drops the S too. Did the government spell his name wrong for most of his life and he was too polite to correct them? Or did Squire have some quiet sort of objection to the S at the end of his name and chose to remove it himself?

One other curious thing about his signature is that it does not resemble the one that features on the modern-day beer brand that bears his name.

Here's the genuine James Squire signature from the marriage certificate

And here's the one the beer brand uses

They don't look that similar, do they? Particularly the surname. Sure, you could suggest the beer brand signature has been embellished to make it look a bit more like a logo and maybe you could be right (though it should be pointed out that the beer brand doesn't claim the logo is his actual signature).

But here's what I'm thinking. I'm thinking someone based it on the signature of the wrong James Squire. See, our man Squire had a son with Elizabeth Mason, who was also called James. He was an executor of his dad's estate and signed several documents relating to the probate.

And here's the signature of Squire Jr

James Squire

You ask me, the way the surname is written looks very similar to the signature on that appears on the beer labels – look at the way the way the Q joins up at the bottom of the U and the fact that the dot for the letter I actually appears over the R. To me it looks like the signature on the beer bottles isn't actually that of Squire's but rather has been based on his son's.

Incidentally, while we know what the real Squire signature looks like, we don't know what the man himself looked like. How tall was he? What colour was his hair? Or his eyes? Was he fat or thin? Did he have a beard? We really don't know. I could find no written description that offers even the slightest bit of information about his physical appearance – though given he appears to have had little trouble finding female companionship we can assume he hadn't been clobbered with the ugly stick. But beyond that, we know bugger all.

Squire doesn't even seem to have bothered to pay someone to paint his portrait either. Squire became a successful businessman who owned a stack of land, so he would have definitely had the money to pay a convict artist. Similarly, by the early 1800s, he was enough of a local identity in the Kissing Point area that it would seem some artist would deem him worthy of a sitting. And yet there is no artistic likeness of him that we know of.

One researcher has engaged in a bit of wishful thinking in suggesting there is in fact a painted likeness of Squire. They point to a painting of Squire's Kissing Point property created by convict artist Joseph Lycett. Technically speaking, the painting is of the Parramatta River, as that takes up almost a third of the canvas, and shows Squire's estate way off in the distance.

On the river is a small sailboat with four people on board. It's claimed that one of those four people is

Squire. The basis of this claim seems to be nothing more than the fact Squire's will mentions a boat he owned called the Lucy (which he would leave to his housekeeper and lover Lucy Harding) There is no evidence to suggest that boat in the foreground – or any of the other four boats that can be seen – is Squire's.

Also, if you look closely at the painting you can see that none of the people in the boat have any facial features. Their heads are just empty circles wearing hats, which makes them useless for gaining any idea of what Squire looked like. Even if is Squire, which it probably isn't.

The painting is dated 1825, which is three years after James Squire died. Its title is *The Property of the Late Mr James Squires* (there's that S at the end of his name again). The date and the painting's title strongly suggest the painting was created after Squire's death. So, unless Squire was a colonial zombie, it seems highly unlikely he's anywhere in this painting.

<u>21</u>
More Than a Feeling

In which some guy named John Boston
arrives in town

October 25, 1794, has become a significant day in the modern-day mythology of James Squire the beer brewer. That day in late October was the day one John Boston arrived in Sydney Cove. Thanks to a passive-aggressive fight between two corporations who each took one of these guys' names for their beer brand, there's a bit of argy-bargy as to who was the country's first brewer. But back in the day itself, Boston's arrival probably meant bugger-all to Squire. And Squire's presence probably meant bugger-all to Boston too.

There's certainly no reference to them ever crossing paths. In fact, six months after Boston's arrival, Squire became a free man and moved away from Sydney Cove to his land grant at Kissing Point. So it's quite plausible they had nothing at all to do with each other – and one may not have ever spoken a single word to the other.

Boston was a bit of a rabble-rouser and trouble-maker back in England. To be honest, when you read some of the things he said (as we will do in the next two chapters), he does come off as a bit of an insufferable bastard. The kind of guy who always thinks he's the smartest person in the room but is too arrogant to realise he's not. Boston was a bit sick of "reactionary" England and the place was probably a bit sick of him too, so him choosing to pack up and head to Sydney was probably seen by both sides as a win.

Despite loathing England and its leaders, Boston didn't seem to think it at all hypocritical to expect them to foot the bill to send him and his family to Sydney ("Yeah, I hate everything you stand for. Now give me some money"). Which is why, in December 1793 he wrote a letter to the Colonial Office in which he talked himself up massively.

"I was brought up a surgeon and apothecary, but have never since followed that profession. I have since made my particular study those parts of chemistry that are more particularly usefull [sic] in trade and business. Have, therefore, a knowledge of brewing, distilling, sugar-making, vinegar-making, soap-making, etc. I have been in business as distiller, but was unsuccessful.

I likewise have a theoretical and some practical knowledge of agriculture."

To me, that reads like the CV of a person who is severely under-qualified for the job but is grabbing onto whatever meagre skills they have in an attempt to try and sound like a decent applicant – and in the process get their CV to go for more than a single page.

Despite this joke of a letter, England agreed to send Boston and his family over. Lieutenant-Governor Francis Grose (who was given charge of the colony when Phillip left and pretty much ran it for himself and his soldiers) received a letter from England in February 1794 in which Boston was described as someone who would "prove particularly useful to the settlement by curing fish and making salt, the objects to which his attention has been particularly drawn".

So Boston and his family came over on the Surprize. And apparently dicked around for almost a year before looking to actually make some salt by extracting it from seawater. You know, that thing he was sent over to do. And, no surprises, he proved to be spectacularly crap at it. Judge Advocate David Collins recorded that, despite having seven convicts at his disposal, Boston only managed "three or four bushels of salt in more than as many weeks".

So he gave up on that and went and made beer,

which he reportedly learned how to do by reading about it in an encyclopaedia on the trip over to Sydney.

His beer, bittered with tomato leaves and stems, seemed popular enough to allow him to build a larger brewery. Though Governor Hunter apparently didn't think much of his brewing skills – or his skills regarding anything beyond being a massive pain in the backside. In 1798, Hunter wrote to the Duke of Portland; "I am of the opinion [he] will continue to be one of those whom the colony will not derive any advantage from". Portland replied that, if Hunter wanted he could give him a choice – bugger off back to England or stop living off the colonial welfare teat.

In time Boston would leave the colony – and one imagines very few people shed a tear. In 1801 he bought a ship called the El Plumier and sailed to the Cape of Good Hope with cargo to sell. But the voyage, like so many other things Boston touched, went pear-shaped. His ship was stolen and it took him until May 1804 before he could get a new ship and return to Sydney. Where everyone went "Oh, God, it's you again."

He got the hint and, after a couple of months, decided to leave on another trading voyage, which again went pear-shaped. He anchored at the island of Tongatapu in Tonga, where the natives seemed friendly. Until he and his crew got ashore, whereby the natives promptly killed them. And, as rumour has it, ate them.

22

First in Line

In which we discuss the whole "who was first" thing

It'd be hard to get out of a biography of James Squire without giving a bit of time to that hoary old argument about whether it was him or Boston who was first. The TL:DR answer? Squire. Squire was first – he was so clearly first that it does my head in that we even talk about Boston being a candidate.

Before we get into the evidence, there are a few explanatory notes. Firstly, the title of "Australia's first brewer" does not mean they were the first person to ever brew a beer in this country. Because if that's the criteria, neither Squire nor that charlatan Boston was first. There are records of beer being brewed on the First Fleet. It was most likely awful but it was definitely beer. Arthur Bowes Smyth, the ship's doctor on board the convict transport Lady Penrhyn, brewed some spruce beer on the way over and left us a recipe in his diary (complete with random capitalisation) – "take 10 gallons of water, lukewarm, eight pounds of molasses (or treacle), Six Table spoonfulls of Essence of Spruce, One pint of Yeast, Stir it well together – it will be fit for bottling in a week & for drinking in a week after".

The good doctor hung around in Sydney until late April and it seems to me quite plausible that he brewed at least one batch on Sydney soil before then. And he wouldn't have been the only one able to knock up a batch. So by the time Squire got around to making beer more than two years after landing in Sydney Cove, there would almost certainly have been people who had done it before him.

Secondly, the title of our first brewer definitely includes what we'd think of today as homebrewers. Because, in the first 10 years of Sydney Cove, *every* brewer would have been making their stuff at home.

Thirdly, they're not making it to get themselves smashed but to sell to others.

Oh, and one other thing. We have to assume the two of them are the only ones in the race and there wasn't some other person lost to history who beat both of them to the punch. The colony was fighting for survival in those early years so it's not as if someone would be preoccupied with taking copious notes about who was brewing beer; they'd be more interested in getting enough food to eat.

The sum total of Boston's joke of a claim comes from an observation made by NSW colony's judge advocate David Collins about the price of a range of goods in Sydney just before he left in September 1796. One of these goods was beer made by Boston, which Collins mentioned in his work *An Account of the English Colony in New South Wales*.

Collins wrote that it was "brewed from Indian corn, properly malted, and bittered with the leaves and stalks of the love-apple, (Lycopersicum, a species of Solarium) or, as it was more commonly called in the settlement, the Cape gooseberry. Mr Boston found this succeeded so well, that he erected at some expense a building proper for the business, and was, when the ships sailed, engaged in brewing beer from the abovementioned materials, and in making soap."

Incidentally, Collins wasn't too crash-hot when it came to identifying plants – the love apple is a tomato, not a cape gooseberry.

In his journal article 'Australia's First Brewer' David Hughes suggests Boston started brewing a bit earlier than late 1796. His paper gives evidence to suggest he and his partners were brewing in their house as early as winter 1795. But even if that is true, then Squire has that beat by more than a year. In his case we have

Squire's own words as to when he started brewing, in his evidence before the Bigge Inquiry in 1819.

"I have been in the colony from its earliest establishment and for 30 years I have been a brewer. At first I lived in Sydney, and brewed beer in small quantities. I sold it then for 4d per quart and made it from some hops that I got from the Daedalus. I also brewed for General Grose and Col Patterson for their own consumption from English malt. I have been established at Kissing Point as a brewer for 28 years, and have brewed beer from Indian corn and colonial barley."

Based on that evidence, Squire was brewing as early as 1789. Now you could mount a case to suggest he was talking about events that happened three decades ago, so he could have been a bit foggy on the exact year he started.

However, there are corroborating details in that statement that help to nail down a time. He said he was brewing for General Francis Grose, who left the colony in December 1794 – less than two months after Boston's arrival. For Boston to have beaten Squire to the title of first brewer, he needed to be brewing as soon as he got off the Surprize, and we know he wasn't doing that at all.

There's also the mention of the ship HMS Daedalus

and that it was carrying hops. Researchers checking the ships logs found the Daedalus delivered 16 cases of essence of malt, seven casks of malt and four casks of hops to Sydney in 1793. That's a year before Boston arrived in Sydney. It's very believable that Squire did use those ingredients – or at least the hops – to make beer. Otherwise, it would see a bit odd that he knew the ship had some on board and would still remember it and be able to mention it to the Bigge Inquiry 30 years later.

That independent evidence points to Squire brewing in 1793 – though he could have started before then. But still, starting in 1793, is early enough to kill off any claim Boston has to being the first brewer.

23
Kill the Pig

In which we hear a tale about Boston far more interesting that whether he was the first to make beer

Outside of the fact that he brewed beer, most people know very little about James Squire, which is a little sad.

It's an even sadder story for Boston, for while he was undoubtedly a bit of a tosser and a pain in the butt, the *only* thing people know about him is that he made some beer. It's sad because there is a far more interesting – and more important story – about Boston, but it seldom gets heard.

And it started with a spot of pig-shooting.

On the morning of October 29, 1795, a neighbour gave Boston some very bad news. It seemed someone had pumped some lead into one of his pigs – "a very fine sow considerably advanced in pig", as Boston would later describe it. The pig had been shot in a nearby patch of ground belonging to Captain Foveaux of the New South Wales Corp.

It had been shot by a soldier, one Private William Faithfull, who was only following the orders of Major Grose. The major had told his men that "all hogs seen in the streets, that are not yoked, and have not rings in their noses, are ordered to be shot", due to the damage they had been doing to property and the colony's vegetable patches.

So Boston, in letting his "fine sow" escape, was in the wrong. Despite this uncomfortable truth, he stormed on the scene full of righteous indignation and shouted "who is the damned rascal who shot my sow?". That was when things went south quite quickly.

Faithfull's superior, Quartermaster Thomas Laycock, looked to his private and said Boston had called him a rascal and so commanded him to give the uppity settler a good thumping. The private moved forward to administer said thumping, when Boston picked up an axe handle. This led Ensign Neil McKeller to tell Faithfull to club Boston with his musket.

Faithfull followed orders, hitting Boston "upon the back of his head with such violence as [it] bent the ramrod and would have undoubtedly produced death if it had fallen upon any other part of the head". Those are Boston's own words, and he was a bit of a drama queen so perhaps he's overstating things a little with that last bit about how it could have killed him.

The whack on the head notwithstanding, Boston was able to get in close to Faithfull and duke it out. The settler won on points, giving the private a bloody nose. As is the case when two guys start punching on, a crowd had formed by this stage. Boston, apparently one for pouring oil on a fire, called all the soldiers a "parcel of rascals" and then told Laycock his actions were those of a rascal.

Laycock ordered another soldier, Private William Eaddy, to thrash Boston. The settler was ready for another fight, saying he would give the soldier a "good licking". It was only the sense of Boston's wife, who was in the crowd, that put an end to the situation by dragging her foolish husband away.

And there perhaps it would have rested had Boston not been a man eternally convinced about how right he was. Just over a month after the incident, he took the audacious move of suing Laycock, McKellar, Faithfull and Eaddy, demanding damages of £500. This was a case that would test the foundations of the colony. Was Sydney simply just a prison and the soldiers the guards who ruled the roost? Or was it a fair society where everyone had the right to seek restitution for their grievances and where even soldiers had to answer for their actions?

Boston himself saw the mere fact that his suit was able to proceed as a sign of the latter, telling the court "the impartial and the dignified conduct of your honours during the trial have proved to the colony that justice is open to all and that none are superior to the laws". Though he did say this before the verdict was handed down, so he might have been sucking up to them a bit.

The judges did lean his way, to a degree. Regarding Laycock and Faithfull, they found Boston's evidence more compelling than theirs and so found them guilty.

"We know that the military is a school of honour – and that no term save that which brands him with the want of courage, can be more harsh in a soldier's ear than that of rascal," the court's verdict stated.

"This however does not amount to a justification of the assault and it is the duty and province of courts of justice to protect from personal outrage all those who are in the King's peace."

But the court awarded Boston far less than the £500 he had been seeking; both soldiers were ordered to pay Boston 20 shillings.

McKellar and Eaddy were let off, the judges saying

nothing against them was proven in court.

Private Faithfull appealed his sentence, perhaps at the urging of Laycock. The private claimed he was just upholding the law and "that a peace officer in England would without hesitation, if called a damned rascal for executing his orders, have levelled the insulting offender at his feet." He went on to suggest the courts should then further punish such an insulting offender.

The appeal was overseen by the new governor John Hunter, who had arrived in the colony shortly before the original assault. He threw out the appeal, saying "the assault complained of has been fully proved and that I do not only confirm the verdict already found by the court in which this case was tried but I must had that I have thought it a lenient one."

Boston no doubt was a bit more insufferable after that finding.

24

More Beer

*In which we try and find out a little about
the beers Squire made*

Through the James Squire beer brand, we've been
told all sort of things – some of them true, some of
them not so much. One thing we've not been told is
what sort of beer he was brewing.

Which is a strange oversight for a company making
beer in his name, don't you think? I do. Though I
wouldn't expect them to brew a beer designed to
replicate Squire's own concoctions because it probably
wouldn't taste the best.

Unlike other brewers, Squire himself did not put
ads in the colony newspaper the *Sydney Gazette* – at
least none that I was able to find. This perhaps
suggests that, by the time the paper began publishing
in the first years of the 1800s, Squire had already made
enough of a success of his Malting Shovel tavern and

brewery at Kissing Point that advertising wasn't required.

This is a small pity, for those ads from other brewers do contain descriptions of the beers they had up for sale. It would have been helpful to have such a list from Squire himself.

Given the time in which Squire was brewing and the country from which he'd just come, I think we can reasonably conclude that Squire was making porter – a dark beer not best suited for the warm Australian climate. In his book about British beers *Amber, Gold and Black*, beer historian Martyn Cornell mentions that porter was carried to Australia on the First Fleet and "by the time it reached Australia, porter had been the dominant style of beer in London for decades, and was drunk in enormous quantities".

There is also the possibility Squire was also making a mild ale, which Cornell describes as "almost the only alternative to porter and stout for most drinkers for more than a century" but it is telling that porter is the only beer style mentioned in journals and correspondence in the early years of the colony. In fact it was the first beer drunk on Australian soil – on the very first day the First Fleet landed at Botany Bay. On that day – January 19, 1788 – Captain Philip Gidley King wrote in his diary of getting into small boats and exploring some of the rivers around the bay. "We went ashore and ate our salt beef and in a glass of porter drank [to] the health of our friends in England".

Also, in 1820, Squire gave evidence to the Bigge Inquiry into the colony, which included a detailed description of his brewing methods. Sadly he chose not to specify what sort of beers he was making. However, when he talked of how much beer he was making and the price, he used "the price of porter imported from England at present" as a benchmark. It would seem strange for him to do that if he himself was not also brewing porter.

So porter was a popular style at the time, there was already a market for it among the beer drinkers in the colony, (and it remained until at least 1820 based in Squire's testimony to the inquiry) so it's a safe assumption that would have been what Squire brewed.

It's also safe to say it probably wasn't that great. It certainly wouldn't have been consistent. Squire's inquiry testimony stated that most of his beers were made with corn rather than barley, and at least some of his brews would have been without hops (perhaps using a similar bittering agent as rival brewer John Boston – the leaves and stalks of a tomato plant).

There is little information about the difficulties of brewing in the first decades of the colony. However, there is information from throughout the 1800s, which describe the problems of consistency. In his paper 'A new drink for young Australia: from ale to lager beer in New South Wales, 1880 to 1930', academic Brett J Stubbs shows that Australian beer in the 1880s was pretty shoddy.

Stubbs quotes from the *Australian Brewers Journal* from the 1880s, which complained that "the greater portion of the beer sold and consumed throughout Australia is really merely 'swipes', 'soft' tasteless, insipid, sugar-and-water sort of stuff, which the Australian working man drinks because he cannot get anything better at a reasonable price".

In the same piece Stubbs writes, "Early Australian brewers … were heavily handicapped by a warm climate and by generally inferior water supplies. In addition their equipment was primitive, raw materials (hops and malt) were often inferior, and highly skilled brewers were unavailable."

TG Parsons in his essay 'The limits of technology – or why didn't Australians drink colonial beer in 1838' points out a similar dodginess with our beer 50 years before the 1880s; "the real point is that given the existing technology, colonial beer was a poor substitute for the English article".

These descriptions of brewing in the 1800s can

safely be taken as a representation of what beer in Sydney Cove in the late 1700s would have been like. The alternative – that Squire nailed how to make great beer in the 1790s but no-one else took any notice and struggled along brewing rubbish for another hundred years – is just farcical.

Contemporary reports of the quality of Squire's beer are virtually non-existent. I have yet to come across any reference from when Squire was alive that describes his beers. In 1827 (five years after Squire's death), Peter Miller Cunningham published two volumes under the absurdly long title of *Two Years in New South Wales; a Series of Letters, Comprising Sketches of the Actual State of Society in that Colony; of its Peculiar Advantages to Emigrants; of its Topography, Natural History etc etc*. Presumably it was two volumes because the title alone took up most of the first one.

Cunningham wrote in that book that "Squire's beer therefore was as well-known and as celebrated in this as Meux and Co's in your hemisphere". Meux and Co was a popular brewery at the time but, these days, is best known for the London Beer Flood of 1814, where huge vats of porter ruptured and more than a million litres of porter spewed out of the brewery and down the streets.

Before you crack wise about how you'd grab a

schooner glass and lean out the window as the torrent rushed past, keep in mind the flood killed people. Eight women and children died; the death toll would have been far greater had the men in those streets not been at work. So not really the light-hearted tale it's so often portrayed as.

Anyway, back to Cunningham's description of Squire's beer. It reads like a second-hand description that someone has given Cunningham and that the author had never had a full cup of the beer in front of him. Cunningham's book offers another possible reference to the quality of Squire's product. He quotes a gravestone of one of Squire's customers in the nearby Parramatta cemetery, which allegedly read "ye who wish to lie here, Drink Squire's beer!". Cunningham – who never met Squire – claims the man himself would joke about the epitaph. If you ask me, it doesn't sound like the epitaph was meant to be a compliment. More a suggestion that Squire's beers might kill you.

The earliest reference to the quality of Squire's brews that I could find was in his obituary in the *Sydney Gazette*. That piece states that his cultivation of hops allowed him "to brew beer of an excellent quality". Though you'd hardly expect them to be disparaging about his beer in the guy's obituary.

A review of Squire's beer in the *Sydney Monitor* of 1831 - nine years after his death – saw no need to shy away from being disparaging.

"Old Mr. Squires, the patriarch of Kissing Point on the Parramatta River, was, twenty years ago, the only brewer in the colony whose name came before the public with any degree of notoriety. When maize or barley were low and sugar high, he brewed from barley or maize malt. But when grain was high, and sugar low, he brewed either entirely from sugar, or from half and half.

"The fame of Squires' beer never rose high in the colony among impartial judges; and of the two, his sugar beer was preferred to his malt beer. The latter very soon acquired a pungent acidity in the throat, which the sugar beer was much slower in contracting."

This description paints Squire as a guy who used whatever ingredients were the cheapest. The statement "when maize or barley were low" is a reference to their prices and it suggests Squire looked more to price than quality when it came to ingredients.

As far as the unnamed author of this article was concerned, Squire was just one example of the problem with Australian beer brewers and beer drinkers. The author said that the beer served in the colony was little more than "fermented sugar and water, impregnated with hops".

"The hopped sweet-wort drunk in Sydney at this time is drawn out of the vat today and tomorrow may be seen at the taps of all the public houses in Sydney. And the newer it is, the better the Sydney folks like it, because it is the sweeter."

Which means to modern palates, Squire's beer would have been hot, flat and sweet. No wonder spirits and ciders were far more popular at the time.

25

Get Free

In which James Squire finishes his seven-year sentence and starts buying land

Okay, now the whole John Boston thing has been put to bed, let's get back to seeing what else was happening to James Squire. By April 1792 he'd served his seven-year stretch for chicken-thieving and so was a free man. From there started a 10-year stretch where it's a bit tricky to work out exactly what he was doing.

Here's one problem – he was freed in 1792 yet didn't get the land grant that went to all emancipated convicts until 1795. However, his Bigge inquiry evidence said he'd been brewing at Kissing Point since 1792, which suggests he moved out there before he had his own patch of land.

In his journal article 'Australia's First Brewer', Hughes puts forward a suggestion that is as good as any. A land grant was made in 1792 to John Chapman Morris, who Squire would have a later connection with due to his serving as administrator on Morris' estate when he died in 1806. Morris apparently didn't work his land – situated in close proximity to the Parramatta River – and so it was forfeited and ended up in the hands of Richard Cheers in September 1792. "It is quite possible that Squire went to Kissing Point in late 1792 to work on Cheers' land, either as an employee or a partner," Hughes wrote.

Hughes also points out that four other land grants on which Squire's Malting Shovel tavern and brewery would later stand were also handed out in 1792. He suggests it's equally plausible that he could have brewed on the properties of any of these four people before getting his own land grant.

One thing seems clear – Squire was unlikely to have shifted his operations to his own 30-acre lot when he got it in 1795. That's because it was further away from the river's edge, cut off by a row of those blocks handed out in 1792. Access to water is vital when it comes to brewing beer so it would see an odd choice for Squire to move away from a riverside spot on Cheers' (or someone else's land) in favour of a block cut off from river access by other properties.

In the three years following his 1795 grant, Squire began acquiring other properties in the area that were not being worked on. In some cases he appears to have paid a token amount far below the actual value to get his hands on the block of land.

This has since been portrayed in a light-hearted way; that Squire was being a bit cheeky by acquiring the properties in this manner. But, viewing it through modern eyes, it all seems a bit underhanded; especially when you consider that rum-drinking was still very popular – and rather expensive. Some convicts had been known to sell food or clothing to get their hands on some booze. Perhaps some of the newly emancipated convicts Squire bought land off had just such a habit.

For them, the offer of a few coins for land they weren't using would have been accepted with glee. That was money that could buy drunkenness for themselves. If this happened then it could be seen as Squire preying on the weaknesses of others to gain an advantage, which is not really "cheeky" by any stretch.

Years later, in 1819, Squire put all his land up for sale and took an ad out in the *Sydney Gazette*. That ad listed the size of each land grant he'd bought as well as who he bought it from. All-up he had picked up a total of 886 acres from 12 other people. Curiously, his own 50-acre grant does not appear in the list, which suggests that he may have sold it. Maps of the land grants in Kissing Point show those he later acquired to be, in large part, connected to each other while his initial grant from 1795 sits all on its own five blocks away. It would seem odd to keep that block but build up a property empire in another area of the township.

Sometime between 1796 and 1798 Squire picked up perhaps the most important land grant in his portfolio – that of John Pollard. These 25 acres were riverfront property and included the point that gave the region its name of Kissing Point. It was where Squire would establish his Malting Shovel tavern and brewery in late 1798, where he would later grow hops and where he would live.

It would also be where he really turned his life around, going from being a convict to a respected man of the region. In this he would show the surprising benefits of being sentenced to transportation. Some, like Squire, recognised that being slung to the other side of the world actually presented them with opportunities they could never have hoped for back home in England. No way could Squire ever have expected to become a land baron had he remained in England.

But in Sydney Cove, where the route from peasant to landowner was far, far shorter and free from hurdles, he could make himself a more wealthy person, a person with a much higher social standing than a chicken-thieving former publican would ever have dreamt.

<u>26</u>
The Stroke

In which James Squire hits the presses for the first time

On March 5, 1803, the *Sydney Gazette* was printed for the first time. The colony's first newspaper, it was published by the government, and editor Robert Howe acknowledged that would limit what would appear in its pages – though he did try and put a positive spin on it.

"The utility of a paper in the colony, as it must open a source of solid information, will we hope, be universally felt and acknowledged," Howe wrote in that first edition.

"We open no channel to political discussion or personal animadversion [that's "criticism" to you and me]. Information is our only purpose."

It took our man Squire four months to get a mention in the *Gazette*. But they made up for it by mentioning him twice in the same issue – July 3, 1803.

While he would become known as a man who did many great things, in that first mention he is a victim. On June 26, 1803, someone stole two of his oars and a boat sail. They seem like odd items to pinch, until you realise someone else's boat went missing that same night. And that a number of convicts suspiciously went missing at the same time.

"It is suspected these depredations have been committed by a party of offenders, consisting of five men now absent from labour at Castle Hill, and J Duce, cockswain of the government long boat," the *Gazette* reported.

The second mention in that same issue was because an escaped convict by the name of Jonathan Horral was caught on his farm.

As for those oar thieves, they were caught days later after trying to smuggle themselves aboard a schooner named the Francis. When they faced trial, the magistrate dismissed the charges of stealing the boat and Squire's oars and sailcloth because it was too hard to get the boat – which would have been the evidence – back to Sydney. Instead they were sentenced with trying to escape.

All were found guilty with the ringleader Duce getting 500 lashes while the others a somewhat less painful 300 lashes each. It is doubtful Squire ever got his oars and sailcloth back.

27

Runaway

*In which Squire deals with a naughty –
and also dumb – convict while being relieved
his sheep are okay*

In 1803 it must have been hard to get good help. A free man, Squire could get convicts assigned to him by the government. It was a good deal for the settlers – they got a supply of labour for the length of the prisoner's sentence and didn't have to pay them a cent. Though, sometimes, you get what you pay for and, in 1803, Squire didn't get a good deal at all.

In April of that year a retired soldier named John Elder appeared before the court for stealing from a youth. In his defence Elder said he committed the crime so he could go on the government stores. The magistrate obliged him – sentencing Elder to two years labour.

Shortly after that time Elder was assigned to Squire,

who put him in charge of the sheep. Elder grew tired of that and, on October 22 he took the flock of 250 sheep and goats out and then simply walked off. The *Gazette* opined that, while a convict escaping was bad, it could have been worse. It was a "misconduct by which much serious injury might have been sustained as well from the loss of the flock, as from their getting in among the wheat of the neighbouring settlers.

"This fortunately however was not the case as the whole about the accustomed hour found their way home without a single straggler deficient." Phew, at least the sheep were okay.

Still, Squire was not happy and offered a 10-shilling reward if someone helped to find Elder. This reward worked, though not in the way you might have expected. Elder, who had been on the run for six weeks, heard about the reward and figured he could turn himself in and claim it. He obviously wasn't a very bright soul – he didn't get the reward but he did get another three months added to his sentence.

It wasn't the last time this "idle and unfortunate character" was in trouble with the law. In March 1804 he was apprehended in the woods near the Hawkesbury River. Without any visible means of support, he was branded a vagrant and sentenced to another six months. Incidentally, in the *Gazette* report of this incident, James Squire is referred to as "R Squires", which perhaps suggests our man wasn't quite that well known at the time.

<u>28</u>

Strange Brew

In which Squire finds the Governor pushing into his territory

In 1804 James Squire and his Malting Shovel Tavern got some competition in the beer brewing stakes from a surprising source – the colonial government. It built its own brewery in Parramatta, on the corner of George and O'Donnell streets, and brewed its first batch of beer in September 1804. But it wasn't a serious threat to Squire; unable to control the rampant theft of beer by brewery employees, the government decided to pull out just a year later.

The decision to brew beer was one Governor Philip Gidley King had been thinking about for a while. With plenty of the populace of the colony still getting stonkered on rum and other spirits, he felt the addition of a beverage lower in alcohol would be a good thing for the colony. It was also the time leading into the so-called Rum Rebellion, (which we don't deal with much here as there's no evidence it had any effect on Squire). The NSW Marine Corps had effected a monopoly on spirits, so the government brewing beer was also seen as a way of breaking the ranking soldiers' control of the alcohol market.

King had been thinking about it as far back as mid-1802 and mentioned his thoughts in correspondence with an MP by the name of Lord Hobart in England, who very much liked the idea.

"The introduction of beer into general use among the inhabitants," Lord Hobart wrote, "would certainly lessen the consumption of spirituous liquors. I have therefore in conformity with your suggestion taken measures for furnishing the colony with a supply of ten tons of porter, six bags of hops, and two complete sets of brewing materials."

He also said he'd get merchant ships to bring out more porter and hop plants when the growing season was suitable.

By May 9, 1803, King's dreams of a brewery were becoming reality. "We are commencing with fixing the materials brought by the Cato [a ship] in a large government building at Parramatta," he wrote to undersecretary Sullivan, "which I have no doubt will succeed and greatly prevent the importation and use of spirits."

By September of that year King was fretting that, while the building was almost finished "we are in want of a proper person" to brew the beer that "will be of infinite advantage to the inhabitants". Yes, it seemed King was putting way too much faith in the qualities of beer.

That problem of finding a brewer was solved in March 1804 when David Collins, now governor in Tasmania, sent King "a man who is a most excellent brewer". A man who planned to bring with him some unnamed roots and leaves from Tasmania that he claimed were very good substitutes for hops. While unnamed, this was likely Thomas Rushton, who has been recorded as the brewer when the brewery opened in September 1804.

Rushton must have been late in arriving because on April 1, King wrote to under-secretary Sullivan that "a small quantity of beer" had been made at the brewery but "unfortunately we have not a professed brewer in the colony". It would appear King wasn't very well-informed – Squire had been brewing for around a decade by this time (though other correspondence from King seems to dismiss Squire as someone who only brewed in "small quantities") and others were making and selling their own beer too. The latter would have been easy for King to discover, given they'd been taking out ads in the *Sydney Gazette* for the past year.

On September 15 the brewery – capable of making 3600 barrels of beer a week – swung into gear. King released a general order on September 25, 1804, that people running licenced premises could buy up to 32 gallons of beer, for which they would be charged a shilling and fourpence per gallon. Commissioned civil and military officers would get five gallons a week and sergeants three gallons at a shilling a gallon. And the settlers? Well it was up to the whims of the governor as to how much they could have. Payment was to be made in "wheat, barley, hops, casks or iron hoops delivered into His Majesty's stores".

In the first month, the brewery put out 2300 gallons of beer a week and in December, King wrote to Lord Hobart claiming success and promising to send over a few bottles. That month, the total output was 4247 gallons, of which the convicts' share accounted for 1345 gallons, the military's 1251 gallons, the settlers received 950 gallons all-up and even the police force got to slake their thirst, being given 105 gallons in the first few months of the brewery's operation.

The success of the government's endeavours to brew beer didn't last. Partially because each employee at the brewery got around four gallons of beer a week. And there were quite a few employees; with perks like that it's not hard to understand why everyone wanted to work there. The free beer wasn't enough, there was apparently widespread theft as well. So King decided to admit defeat and, by 1806, looked to lease out the brewery to Rushton for two years. The lease was free, as long as he abided by a series of conditions, which included supplying "200 gallons of strong beer per month to the governor" for use of the convicts.

Rushton chose not to renew the lease and an ad in the *Sydney Gazette* in June 1808 announced he had started brewing at the Brickfields (between Circular Quay and Central stations).

He didn't last there long either – less than a year later the Brickfields brewery was being let out. It did come with the offer that "any person wishing to take the same who may not be conversant in malting and brewing, the proprietor has no objection to give such needful instructions, as if pursued, cannot fail of making good beer".

The government's brewery in Parramatta appears never to have made another batch of beer after Rushton left.

<u>29</u>

House of Fun

In which we discover the Malting Shovel Tavern may not have been a place to take the kiddies

There are a number of stories about how Kissing Point got its name. The most popular revolve around the boats that navigated up and down Parramatta River. One version says it was the furthest up the river heavily-laden boats could go before their hulls "kissed" the sandy bottom. The other version claims it was because the boats used to "kiss" the point as they went by it. If you look at maps of the region, that latter explanation doesn't seem to pan out as there is plenty of space for ships to navigate around the point without having to get so close to the shore.

Another tale is that Governor Hunter would take his wife up there for picnics, during which he would steal a kiss. There's also the darker origin that the region was so named as a delicate reference to the prostitutes that plied their trade at the point. As much as I like the darker story, that's unlikely to be the origin as the name "Kissing Point" appears while the area is sparsely populated and lacking in many male customers for the ladies. However, it could have served as later reinforcement for the name.

Not long after it opened the Malting Shovel Tavern was one of the places these women would go to work, seeing as how it was a meeting point for men coming and going along the river. It was also a place known for its criminal element, according to Reverend Samuel Marsden's testimony to the Bigge Inquiry. In giving evidence of the morality of the female convicts Rev Marsden was asked if those who had been sent up the Parramatta River complained of ill-treatment. "They generally stopped at Squire's public house, when they got drunk and were robbed," he answered.

The reverend was no fan of taverns in general, believing there were far too many in the colony. "It has always been a drunken country," he told the enquiry, "and I think that the vice of drunkenness is much encouraged by the number of licenced houses."

Squire's pub was also not far from an area of concern to the magistrates in 1805, due to someone having the temerity to brew beer without a licence.

"In consequence of the various complaints that have lately occurred at Parramatta," the *Gazette* reported, "owing to the private breweries which infest the settlement, the magistrates have been under the necessity of removing the cause (so that the effect will in all probability follow) by ordering the private brewer to desist from his unauthorised labours and no beer be vended but by licence."

30

I Will Follow

In which District Constable James Squire
makes Australian police history

When it came to policing the colony, the Night Watch only lasted 10 years before it was scrapped due to a rise in "nocturnal robberies" as Governor Hunter described them. He figured the convicts in the Night Watch were either fat and hopeless or actually the ones engaging in the nocturnal robberies.

The job of protecting the colony then fell to the district constables, a rank that had been set up in 1796 to work alongside the Night Watch. And it wasn't without its dangers, as evidenced by the fate of Constable Joseph Luker – the first police officer in NSW to be killed in the line of duty. Constable Luker was a convict who came to Sydney on the Third Fleet in 1791 and who joined the force in 1796 after serving out his sentence.

In the early hours of August 26, 1803, Constable Luker had been patrolling a recent hotspot for robbery known as Back Row East (the area now bordered by a trio of streets named for former governors – Phillip, Hunter and Macquarie – and Martin Place).

That morning, the constable's body was found in the area. It was a gruesome sight indeed; "a breathless corpse, shockingly mangled, and with the guard of his cutlass buried in his brain," reported the *Sydney Gazette*.

"On the head of the deceased were counted sixteen stabs and contusions; the left ear was nearly divided; on the left side of the head were four wounds, and several others on the back of it. The wretch who buried the iron guard of the cutlass in the head of the unfortunate man had seized the weapon by the blade, and levelled the dreadful blow with such fatal force, as to rivet the plate in the skull, to a depth of more than an inch and a half."

That same night, the home of prostitute Mary Breeze has been broken into. Figuring there was a connection, police rounded up suspects. One of them, a Joseph Samuels, admitted to the robbery and named his accomplices, which included two constables; Isaac Simmonds and William Bladders. Samuels, Constables Simmonds and Bladders, and two other crims named Richard Jackson and James Harwicke, faced trial over the murder. Samuels and Harwicke were found guilty of the murder and sentenced to hang.

On the scaffolding, Harwicke was reprieved but not Samuels – who used his last words to claim Constable Simmonds confessed to him that he had killed Luker. When it came time for the hangman to do his work, he did it very poorly. The rope broke in the middle on the first attempt and Samuels crashed face-first onto the ground. A new rope was brought in but that came loose and Samuels slowly slid down until his feet reached the ground. A third rope also snapped and Samuels fell again. The crowd watching this farce grew angry and demanded a reprieve, which the governor eventually gave.

In the end the murder of Constable Luker went unpunished. This case was well-known in the colony but it didn't seem to stop Squire from signing on as the district constable at Kissing Point. Perhaps he needed the extra cash. He was in the role in January 1805, which was when his law-enforcing exploits made the local paper.

In what was obviously a slow news day for the *Gazette*, it chose to report on Squire's pursuit and capture of "a couple of modern Egyptians" on the "vehement suspicion of sheepstealing". Later that year, there was another somewhat mundane case, where Squire caught an Abraham Smith for thieving from the house of a J Newton. The homeowner seems to have been a repeat victim of a gang of burglars who had "taken themselves to the woods from an aversion to labour, and a preference to a life of profligacy under perpetual apprehension and anxiety". In other words, they found stealing stuff to be easier than working.

Of Squire's cases recorded in the pages of the *Sydney Gazette*, the one that appeared in the edition of July 21, 1810, was the high point of his policing career. It marked the first recorded instance of an Aboriginal tracker helping to track down the bad guys.

Early on the morning of Saturday, July 14, a trio of "armed ruffians" – labourers Patrick McKane, John White and Edward McHugh – broke into the house of Kissing Point resident Richard Jenner. Finding only Jenner's wife and a servant at home, the gang "exercised much violence" towards them before tying them up and then ransacking the house of clothes, cash and "sundry other property".

Squire was called to the scene and could not make any headway for the first two days. At a loss, he brought in a young Aboriginal man by the name of Bundle to see what he could uncover. After walking around the house and the property, Bundle found a footprint with two prominent marks in the sole.

Following these prints, Bundle led Squire to a nearby hut where they found a pair of shoes, one with two nails in the sole that were the source of those distinctive marks.

The owner swore he had nothing to do with the break-in and assault; he had loaned his boots to McKane the night before. Squire, with Mrs Jenner and her servant in tow, then went to McKane's hut in Lane Cove. As soon as she laid eyes on him, Mrs Jenner identified McKane as one of the men in her house that night.

McHugh and White were caught soon after and the trio were found guilty. They appealed and, in October 1810 the appeals court said "Nah, you're still guilty". McHugh, "the most atrocious offender" in the eyes of the court, was sentenced to 100 lashes and two years' hard labor while McKane and White received 50 lashes and a year's hard labour.

31
Hop, Skip, Jump
In which we look at the claim that Squire
was the first to grow hops in the colony

Hops. While you can make beer without them, it certainly tastes better with them. For the first decade or so of brewing in Sydney, the hops came from England by ship. And really, there's no telling what they'd be like after six months at sea. But they'd surely have tasted better than the tomato stalks and leaves or whatever else they'd been using as a bittering agent.

Squire himself had been using imported hops as far back at 1790 when he began brewing with a shipment that came in on the Daedelus. There are also references to hop deliveries in correspondence between various governors and the home country. For example, in 1803 Governor King wrote to Lord Hobart about hops that came via a ship called the Glatton. King had not long before announced plans to build a government brewery but decided these hops would not keep until the construction was finished and so "in the meantime I have allowed a man who has always brewed on his own account to purchase a part of the hops arrived by the Glatton". That man was quite likely Squire.

It wasn't just the hops that were an issue for brewers – finding good-quality barley also posed problems. In his testimony to the Bigge inquiry in 1820 Squire said he had done much of his brewing with corn.

"This grain vegetates better in the warm season," he said. "I have brewed almost entirely from Indian corn as the barley is so bad." He also said that six bushels of English barley were equal to 10 of colonial barley, so he needed more of the locally-grown stuff to make the same quantity of beer.

There was also the problem of barley-growing settlers picking it too early in order to make some cash from it. In a November 1804 order published in the *Sydney Gazette*, Governor King noted "that some of the settlers in the district of Hawkesbury are reaping their barley before it is ripe with a view to putting the same into the store, which will evidently defeat the intention of supplying the inhabitants with beer, as malt cannot be made from barley thus reaped". So he decreed people had to give a sample of the barley before the stores would accept it. The sample would be assessed and rejected if unsuitable.

In regards to hops, Squire eventually took to trying to grow his own at his lands at Kissing Point. It's an endeavour that has seen him credited as the first to grow the green cone-shaped things in the country. It's a conclusion drawn via what I think of as "the cow story".

In January 1805 the *Gazette* reported that Squire had "produced an excellent specimen, consisting of several very fine bunches" of hops. Two months later, he was called before Governor King to show him some hop vines.

"On a vine from last year's cutting were numbers of very fine bunches; and upon a two years old cutting the clusters, mostly ripe, were innumerable, in weight supposed to yield at least a pound and a half, and of a most exquisite flavour."

As a reward for Squire's "unremitted attention" in growing the hops, he was given a cow from the government herd. That offer of a cow would have been welcomed by Squire. It would have been a handy replacement for the one he lost a few months earlier. According to the *Gazette*, Squire's cow found a tub of grains for brewing and ate so much she died three hours later. "When the carcass was opened, a quantity of grains little less than three bushels was found". Five days later, Squire's other cow also fell ill, perhaps from the same issue of grain over-eating, according to the local paper. Her fate was not reported.

Later in March 1805 Squire made a beer with those hops he had presented to the governor and the *Gazette* reported that "their excellence very far exceeds his most flattering expectation". But he may have been a little biased.

There are two things worth noting about the cow story that appears in the *Sydney Gazette*. Firstly, it never says Squire was the first to grow hops (and nor does Squire himself make that claim in his 1820 testimony to the Bigge Inquiry). And secondly, there's a section of the *Gazette*'s story – which is generally not quoted – that clearly shows Squire was not alone when it came to growing hops in Sydney Cove.

"The properties of this valuable plant strongly recommend its culture, to which several of our colonists have applied themselves with laudable and unremitting perseverance."

Which certainly leaves the door open to it being someone else, and not Squire, who deserves the tag of the colony's first hop grower. After all, one of those other colonists could have beaten our man to the punch. If it isn't Squire, then the hop grower's name is lost to history. The only other hop grower I found that was mentioned by name in Squire's lifetime was the former brewer at the government brewery, Thomas Rushton. However, a report in the *Sydney Gazette* rules him out; he became a hop farmer in 1811 – almost a decade after Squire.

But a report in the *Gazette* made harvesting time at Rushton's farm in 1811 seem like an awful lot of fun. "This last gathering was performed by a number of bonny lasses who volunteered their services, and performed their chearing [sic] task with smiles that gave to the countenance a sweetness of expression, not otherwise to be depicted than as the liveliest contrast nature has afforded, to the bitter flower of which they were dismantling the vines."

Based on references to Squire's growing efforts in the *Gazette* and governors' correspondence to and from England, it seems he began growing his own hops in 1803. Those same letters appear to point to someone else growing hops at the same time – or even before – Squire.

In September 1803, Governor King wrote to Lord Hobart, begging him to send regular supplies of hops by ship. "The plant is growing very luxuriantly from some seed brought in by accident last year, and there is no doubt will in time do well, but as not more than 10 plants were raised, many years must elapse before they can be put into use."

It's unlikely to be Squire who grew these, as all published references to his efforts state they came from cuttings and not seeds. Perhaps it was even these plants from which Squire got his own cuttings.

One possibility for the identity of the mystery hop grower, is George Suttor. He arrived in the colony in November 1800 with a collection of plants Sir Joseph Banks had placed in his care. A man with an interest in gardening, perhaps he put that to use in cultivating the first hops in the country.

In March 1804, King again wrote to Hobart about these plants, stating "there are now about forty thriving hops plants growing from a quantity of seed brought by an officer in 1802, which are taken much care of."

If these hops were already growing "very luxuriantly" in late 1803, there is a chance they predate the start of Squire's agricultural efforts. It's not definitive proof that Squire wasn't the first but it does offer enough detail to suggest his claim to that title is by no means clear-cut.

Regardless of who was first, it is clear Squire's brewing was outpacing his hop-growing. He told the

Bigge inquiry he had "seven or eight acres of hops" from which he had harvested half a ton the previous year. He had taken to giving away hop cuttings for other people to grow so that he could then buy their harvest. In 1809 he placed an ad in the *Gazette* claiming he had "from 12 to 1500 plants to spare" and was looking to sell them off.

Despite both growing his own and getting others to grow some for him by 1819 Squire was still well short of the amount of hops he needed. So much so that he asked Governor Macquarie to get England's help.

In a request to Lord Bathurst, Macquarie asked that Squire "be permitted to import about a ton of hops from England in one of the convict ships coming out hither, free of freight, in order to enable him to prosecute his brewing business with more advantage". At the end of the letter Macquarie added a slight backhander to the hop-growing efforts of Squire and others, stating that while there were "considerable quantities" grown they were "as yet much inferior to the English hops".

In response, Bathurst said he would give Squire his freight-free hops but added that he should not ask to do it again as it gave the brewer an unfair competitive advantage.

32

Hey Stoopid

*In which the author takes a brief interlude
for a tale that made his inner child snigger*

From its start in 1803, the *Sydney Gazette* is a great
source for the goings-on in the colony – big and
small. The small things are often the ones that draw
the eye, because they're the bits most historians
writing books don't bother wasting their time on.

A man like Squire appears numerous times in the
Gazette for all manner of things – though not in the
form of an ad for his beer or brewery.

Squire (or Squires as the paper calls him until it
drops the second S in 1820) rated mentions in the
Gazette for police work, efforts at growing hops,
wanting people to get off his land, offering rewards
for stolen items, acting as executors on people's wills
and even, as we have seen when one of his cows eats

leftover grain from brewing and dies.

The January 22, 1809, edition of the *Gazette* features one of those small mentions of Squire. He placed a classified ad for a lost horse; an aged brown mare with a long tail. Anyone "restoring her", as he put it, would be rewarded with one guinea. If someone kept the horse after this notice appeared they would be prosecuted.

It's the name of the horse that amuses me, and is the only reason to repeat this story. Squire chose to call the nag Kicking Fanny.

33
Love Will Tear Us Apart
In which Squire loses someone close to him

While Squire's life changed from that of a convict to a landholder, publican, constable and respected member of the Kissing Point community, there had been one constant – Elizabeth Mason.

They'd met sometime in late 1791, not long after she'd gotten off the boat in Sydney Cove. A year later, they had their first child, Priscilla – whom Squire appeared to initially hide his paternity. But he had no issue with claiming fatherhood of any other children Elizabeth bore.

And she bore quite a few – a further six in fact. Some of the names chosen for their children call back to the family he left behind in England. The second-born daughter shares the name Martha with Squire's English wife, and it's the same story with two of his English-born children – Squire would have a son named James and a daughter named Sarah in both countries.

Squire never divorced Martha Quinton, and he didn't marry any of the women he lived and had children with in Sydney. You can read into that whatever you wish – I like to think it suggests a lasting affection for Martha that even miles of ocean and the passing of years never quite overcame.

Still, the relationship Squire had with Mason was easily the longest of his life. They were together for 18 years, until she passed away on June 10, 1809. The death must have surely weighed heavily on Squire – she had been with him for roughly one-third of his life.

Some choose to cheapen things here by suggesting Squire was having an affair with a servant Lucy Harding while living with Mason. I could find absolutely no contemporary reference to this relationship, and no secondary source that makes the claim of an affair offers any evidence to support it either. It seems to have been held onto because the idea that he had a mistress makes Squire a bit of a rogue, a scoundrel and adds to the image of him as a bit of a pantsman.

It is true that Squire would have a relationship with Harding after Mason's death, but that is certainly not proof of anything happening between the two while

Mason was alive. They may well have been sleeping together but, until I see evidence to support that, I'm dismissing the whole idea of an affair.

34

Go West

In which it is shown that being a small brewer in Australia has always been tough

If you talk to enough craft brewers today, it seems as though the beer industry has a real problem when it comes to paying its debts. Brewers will tell you about the bar that was so eager to get their hands on a few kegs of the cool new beer but strangely slow when it came time to paying for them.

Maybe a bottle shop took a pallet-load of beers, sold them all but the brewery is still yet to see a cent. Or maybe they'll tell you about that beer festival they took part in where the organisers stiffed them at the end of the day. In at least one instance I heard, the organiser took the money and shot off overseas.

It leads one to think that everyone in the Australian brewing industry owes everyone else. And that's really nothing new. Australian brewers have been getting shafted like this for more than 200 years. One of the first – if not *the* first – to get screwed over was convict brewer and publisher Absalom West.

He placed an ad in the *Sydney Gazette* on October 22, 1809, to announce his new brewery near Dawes Point. He was selling strong beer and table beer "and yeast supplied to bakers and private families".

Then, on December 17, 1809, Absalom posted the classified ad (complete with random capitals) in the *Gazette* that likely was the cause of his later problems.

"Absalom West respectfully informs the Public in general, that he will have open for Sale the ensuing week, 20 or 30 Hogsheads of the best Strong Beer; which for the accommodation of purchases will be sold by the Hogshead. Three months Credit will be given on approved security."

Ah yes, it seems Absalom shouldn't have bothered extending anyone credit and instead insisted on cash up front for those hogsheads. Because the next we hear of Absalom West in the pages of the *Sydney Gazette* is in July 1810, where he is calling on his debtors to show him the money. "All those persons who stand indebted to me are requested to step forward and settle their accounts immediately, to prevent me from having recourse to legal measures," his notice in the paper read.

Enough of them must have paid up, for he was still in business in early 1811 - he was successful in getting a spirit licence (all sellers of alcohol in the colony needed a licence to sell spirits. They needed a second one to sell beer – and the *Gazette* carried the names of all of those who were licenced, presumably in the hope it would weed out those in the sly grog business). But by March 1811, things seemed to have taken a turn for the worst for Mr West, with people again not paying up. He placed another notice in the *Gazette* and, for some strange reason, West chose to write it as a poem.

"Absalom West
Does hereby request,
That all who last year
Took on credit his beer,
Whose flavour and strength,
To perfection at length
By Labour and thought
'tis, acknowledged he's brought,
Their debts will discharge,
To let him at large
From claims which no doubt,
Every brewer of stout,
Would his conscience acquit,

> If his assets permit.
> It is therefore declared
> That no one will be spared
> From appearance at Court
> ('tis the last resort)
> Who do not to Absalom's quickly repair,
> And pay what they owe on account of his beer,
> No favour to any one; Soul will be show
> So they'd better save trouble - and pay what they
> owe"

By October 1812, West has had enough of selling beer – and writing poetry – and put his home, a malthouse and brewhouse in Cambridge St, Dawes Point up for sale. There must not have been many takers because it was still on the market in January 1813, and West had added furniture and kitchen utensils to the sale.

West was in a hurry to get his affairs settled because he was planning to head back to England on a ship named the Minstrel, as a May 1813 notice stated. But he must have missed that boat for, in March 1814, West is still in the colony, still asking people to pay up and still threatening to leave (this time on a ship called the Seringapatam). This time he was going, for sure, and told people fellow brewer Thomas Rushton would be collecting his debts.

The struggling brewer (and printer, by the way, who published two books featuring artwork showing views of Sydney) must have made it out for the *Sydney Gazette* never mentions him again. That is, if we assume the Absalom West who surfaces in 1825 is a different person altogether. And we probably should, for this Absalom West showed a penchant for getting in trouble with the law.

In March 1825 this other West was pinged for a bit of B&E, stealing "a keg of spirits, (containing about 5 gallons), a silver watch, nine cheeses, and other articles" from a dwelling at the Brickfields, which was in the vicinity of the suburb of Haymarket.

"The premises had been broken and entered at the back part," the *Sydney Gazette* reported, "and the prisoners being suspected, were watched by Grace Richards, who saw one of them with the keg on his shoulder at a short distance from their house, in company with the other, and when challenged with the robbery, the keg was brought back and left on the premises with very little of its contents absent."

The following year this West again ran afoul of the law for selling spirits without a licence at the race course. "Although the evidence was not sufficiently conclusive to bring the fact home to the prisoner," the

Gazette reported, "yet, as it appeared that he had been known to keep a disorderly place for the reception of persons of loose and suspected character, the Bench ordered him to be returned to Government labour."

While Squire's brewing efforts certainly outlasted those of both Absalom West and the government, they were far from the only rivals he faced in the Sydney beer market. Squire may well have been brewing for more than a decade before he opened the Malting Shovel Tavern on the banks of the Parramatta River, but others came to realise there was some money to be made in beer.

When one of these rivals opened up shop, they often placed a notice in the *Sydney Gazette* – a fact that gives us a great way to track the brewers in the colony. Rosetta Stabler had an eating house unimaginatively called The Eating House that moved around the colony a bit. By the time it moved to Pitts Row (now Pitt Street) in December 1803, her husband William had added his beer to the menu. His ad in the paper promised "prime strong beer which he has brewed of superior strength and quality".

Hawkesbury district constable Andrew Thompson was supplied with brewing utensils for doing his job and being a top bloke (yes, seriously). In an article in

May 1806, he was rewarded for "saving of the lives and much of the property of the sufferers by the repeated floods in that quarter, as well as from his general demeanour". The government-supplied brewing kit came with some conditions; Thompson couldn't sell the beer for more than the set price and he couldn't sell massive amounts to single sellers (avoiding a rum-like monopoly) but instead make sure the distribution is "as general as possible".

By June 1808 Thomas Rushton, the brewer who had been working at the government brewery announced he'd set up digs at the Brickfields. His ad made sure to point out he'd bought the entire supply of hops that came in on a recent ship and had locked in future supplies so that "he will be enabled to continue the brewery without interruption, and to comply with all orders with which his numerous friends may favour him".

Enoch Kinsela chose to inform the beer drinkers of Sydney Cove that he had totally nailed the whole brewing thing. In January 1809, the not-at-all modest Mr Kinsela wished to "acquaint the public that he has at considerable expense, and by many experiments, established the true system of managing the grain of this climate, in its different stages, for producing a strong, clear, wholesome and durable beer".

He managed to stay in business for at least two years – another ad appeared in 1811. A propos of nothing, Enoch didn't like people telling fibs about him; in 1813 he took out a notice in the *Gazette* that he was looking for the person who had been telling porkies about him selling his home and hotel, as he was "determined, on proof, to prosecute the offender or offenders as far as the law will admit".

Other competitors in the beer market included Gregory Blaxland (who also led a crossing of the Blue Mountains) and Benjamin Hill, who was brewing spruce and ginger beers. In touting those beers Hill didn't think he had to say anything about their quality but just saying "all the cool kids drink the stuff" would be enough. In 1820 he claimed "from the very liberal encouragement he has hitherto experienced from most families of respectability in Sydney, that he need not endeavour to explain the beneficial effects of such wholesome beverage".

<u>35</u>

Peaches

*In which we discover another alcoholic
beverage popular with the locals*

These days, cider attracts those with a sweet tooth; usually a younger drinker who has spent years drinking super-sweet soft drinks or those pointless "energy" drinks, so their palate constantly screams for sugar. Some of the ciders these days seem so full of sugar that you could stand a spoon upright in a glass of the stuff. These kids want to get drunk but they don't want their drink to taste like, you know, alcohol – so sugary ciders it is.

That said, it's not the first time Australians turned to cider to get themselves bent. The same thing went on back in Squire's day, when farmers needed to find a way to get rid of a glut of peaches and people needed to find a cheap way to get drunk – so it was a mutually beneficial arrangement.

And one that, curiously, the government didn't like – despite initially encouraging everyone to make the damn stuff.

In March 1805, the *Gazette* was full of praise for those who had worked out how to turn the fruit into booze "in such quantities as to promise real advantage".

"Several of the settlers at Kissing Point have devoted much attention to the praiseworthy object; one of whom informs us that he has already put up about 200 gallons which, with a few months fermentation, he doubts not will be found equal to the apple cyder in strength and not inferior to the taste."

The article then proceeded to go into some detail about how he managed to extract the juice. Really, it's almost as if the *Sydney Gazette* actually wanted people to set up stills and make peach cider.

Of course, they didn't actually want that – you needed to get a government licence to make beer or spirits – but telling people how to make cider and then not expecting them to do it is just weird. At least a decent amount of Sydneysiders thought so too, because what soon followed was an ongoing issue of people cranking out cheap peach-flavoured booze.

In April 1806, the *Gazette* reported that "several

very indifferent characters among the settlers entice the servants of their neighbours from their duty by the lure of cyder made from peaches". What they were getting at was people setting up sly grog houses and getting people drunk; so the law said it would punish both the home owner as well as all the convicts drinking there. Even those with a licence had to prevent "any unlawful or improper meetings of the idle and dissolute in their respective houses".

A month later, on May 11, 1806, there was a report of the case of James Meyne, busted for being in possession of a still. Meyne denied the charge, which did him no good at all – most likely because he had at least 400 gallons of peach cider fermenting at the time in preparation for it to be turned into something stronger.

In June, there was another still uncovered at North Rocks, just off the Parramatta River. The people sent to raid it were watching the two men working the still and, while discussing how to capture them, found the bootleggers unknowingly walking in their direction – so pistols came out and arrests were made.

"On further search being immediately ordered," the *Gazette* reported, "seven casks of cyder were found, containing numerous ingredients to promote fermentation, etc, together with a few quarts of pernicious spirit, concealed in the cavity of a rock."

The search also uncovered information which led to another still being found at the Field of Mars (a brilliant name for an area in the vicinity of Ryde).

The anonymous *Gazette* writer then proceeded to weigh into cidermakers and distillers at some length.

"The activity of Government in restraining this infamous practice, which is certainly a most atrocious attack upon the health of the inhabitants, will, it is to be hoped, very soon effectually suppress every inclination to attempt it.

"The rewards held out for the purpose of bringing the delinquents forward are a sufficient testimony of the most serious determination to crush the evil, by placing every principal in the power of his meanest assistant or associate; and as the principals, agents, and devisers can be esteemed in no other light than as the mercenary factors of pestilential calamity, actuated by a principle of self advantage to spread disorder and contamination, it becomes a public duty assiduously to promote detection, as the only probable means of effectually subduing the evil, and suppressing the dangerous evaporation of so malevolent a spirit."

Fighting words, right? The paper had had enough of people making cider and then turning it into something rougher, right? Surely, they wouldn't then go and do something that appeared to encourage people to make it again, right?

Wrong. Just five months after that screed the *Gazette* published a 450-word explanation on how to pick, store, prepare and ferment peaches. Here's a sample to show just how much detail the article gave.

"Most are already aware, that the juice will ferment without any assistance from yeast or other ingredients; and it is necessary to be known that this state of natural fermentation must not be checked, but allowed to subside of itself, which will be known by the head flattening.

"It must now be drawn into clean and sweet vessels, the neglect of which occasions many a failure; for if it be suffered to remain in the casks in which it fermented, it is not possible to insure it against fermenting anew upon a change in the atmosphere."

Really, it's like they actually wanted people to make cider. In December, they even turned it into a contest where people were asked to make two hogsheads of cider and, after a taste test the following year, the winner would get a cow from the government stores.

It is all evidence of a really odd approach to alcohol regulation - the government makes it illegal to create booze but also spends a good deal of time telling the public how to make the base ingredient of that booze.

36
Don't Tear it Down
In which we find Squire hated it when uninvited visitors turned up

While Squire has been tagged as a very generous man, one who could have died with heaps more money had he not given so much away, that generosity didn't extend to those who dared to sneak onto any of his properties.

From 1806 through to his death in 1822 Squire placed a number of warnings in the *Gazette* telling people to stay the hell off his land. That first notice in 1806 carried with it a tone of frustration on the part of Squire – as well as an ability to take forever to get to the point.

"Persons having repeatedly trespassed on the undermentioned farms – my property – on pretext of an authority to which upon minute enquiry they had no pretention, and having taken timber therefrom without my permission, I do hereby caution any person (unless for Crown purposes) from hereafter cutting down, barking or removing any timber thereform, on pain of prosecution." Additionally, those who spilled the beans on timber thieves operating on any of Squire's properties listed in the warning would get a £5 reward.

It might seem petty on the part of Squire, but timber thievery was rife at the time. A number of other property owners – including the government – had to post a notice to tell people to leave their trees alone.

The timber thieves must have hit Squire hard in early 1811 because in May of that year he placed the same notice for three straight weeks bemoaning the "considerable amount" of timber that had been cut down from the land grants now in his possession and offered that £5 reward to anyone who would dob in the perpetrators so the courts could deal with them.

It wasn't just people thieving timber Squire disliked, it was also those letting their livestock roam onto his land. In 1819 he noted that "herds of horned cattle and other stock have of late been trespassing on my farms and lands against my express orders". He again outlined the lands that were his and if he found cattle on any of his properties after the date of the notice that "I am determined to prosecute such offenders who may have them in their charge with the utmost rigour of the law".

There appears to be no record in the *Gazette* of even one person being prosecuted for either timber thievery or running stock on Squire's land. Which means all Squire's longwinded anger and promises of £5 rewards were for nought.

37
Blackfella Whitefella

In which Squire gets along better than most with the native population

A good number of the early settlers had a lot of time for the native population. As long as that time was spent trying to shoot them, kidnap them or drive them off the land.

We've already seen how even the most benevolent of chaps in Governor Phillip in the end threw all his toys out of the pram and ordered a bunch of them to be killed – partially because of his desire to collect a few heads to send off to his mate Sir Joseph Banks back in England.

But some of the settlers liked the Aboriginal people. Some liked them a whole lot; like Lieutenant William Dawes, who compiled a dictionary of the Eora language with the help of Aboriginal girl Patyegarang. It seems Patyegarang went above and beyond the call, judging by some of the phrases included in Dawes' book. For some reason, he saw the need for people to know the Eora translations for phrases like "to tickle under the armpit", "We shall sleep separate" and "put out the candle Mr D". It would seem Mr D was *exceptionally* friendly with some members of the local population.

James Squire didn't go to that extent but he did appear to get along with those natives who walked his land at Kissing Point (as long as they weren't stealing his timber, one would assume). The most notable among them was Bennelong, who we last met when he was orchestrating the spearing of Arthur Phillip at Manly Cove. Phillip seems to have gotten over that slight for, when he left in 1792, he took Bennelong back to England with him. Though he also took back some kangaroos and dingoes, so one does wonder if Bennelong was on that ship as friend or Antipodean cargo.

He wasn't quite the oddity some in England may have expected. Perhaps that was because Bennelong was already westernised to a degree and no longer fit the English idea of the savage. Or perhaps it was because the English had been invading so many countries that the novelty of seeing a native from far-flung lands had kind of worn off.

Bennelong returned to Sydney in 1795 and despite

later claims he was a man stuck between two cultures but accepted by neither, it seems he did form a clan that hung out along the Parramatta River between Parramatta and Kissing Point. Which is where he came across Squire, who let Bennelong walk across his land and even apparently live on it for a time.

Bennelong died on Squire's estate on January 2, 1813. It has been suggested he fell into a vat of Squire's beer and drowned but to me that sounds like a myth designed to play into the "drunken Aboriginal" stereotype. He was getting old – he was nearly 50 at the time of his death – and had a lot of wounds from previous battles so it seems more likely that's what got him in the end. Squire had Bennelong buried in the garden on Squire's property.

The story goes that he was buried with his wife Boorong, though I cannot find any indication of when she died – though I'd assume it was later that same year.

Squire placed a plaque over the place where Bennelong lay; which was a whole lot more respect than the *Sydney Gazette* could be bothered showing. It gave the guy an awful kicking in an exceptionally nasty obituary.

"The principal officers of government had for many years endeavoured, by the kindest of usage, to wean him from his original habits and draw him into a relish for civilised life; but every effort was in vain exerted and for the last few years he has been but little noticed. His propensity for drunkenness was inordinate; and when in that state he was insolent, menacing and overbearing.

"In fact he was a thorough savage, not to be warped from the form and character that nature gave him by all the efforts that mankind could use."

Eight years later, on July 31, 1821, the visiting Lieutenant Allen Francis Gardiner witnessed what he called a "native fight" on Squire's land. It was more likely a corroboree which included an element of ritual combat afterwards. It is believed that one of the participants was Nanbaree, who as a child had been taken from the beach suffering from smallpox and eventually "adopted" by the surgeon White. The surgeon chose to give him the more English name of Andrew Sneap Hammond Douglass White.

After staying in Sydney Cove for a few years, Nanbaree eventually returned to his countrymen and may well have been seriously injured in that ritual combat on Squire's land on the last day of July in 1821. This is because he died just two weeks later on August 12, his obituary in the *Gazette* stated that he died "at the residence of Mr James Squire", which hints at the possibility of Squire nursing the man through his last days on Earth.

That obituary also suggests an ongoing relationship between the two men.

"Mr Squire, we have every reason to believe, treated him with particular tenderness, and had recourse to many stratagems to rescue him from wretchedness; and, with this view, occasionally gave him amusing employment, accompanied by plenty of indulgence but all proved unavailing – ancestral habits being too indelibly engendered ever to be eradicated by human effort, however strained in its benevolent design."

Before his death he requested to be buried in the same grave as Bennelong and Boorong, a wish Squire fulfilled.

<u>38</u>
Friends
In which we hear the tale of Patrick Troy

In 1810 a man named Patrick Troy wandered into the garden of a Mr Wilson of Waterford County in England. He confronted the man in the garden and demanded his guns. Troy's words probably didn't make Wilson want to co-operate, but the blunderbuss his accomplice was holding surely would have.

The crime all went pear-shaped when the servants inside Wilson's house realised what was happening and locked the doors. Troy and his accomplice yelled at them through a window to open them up again, while Wilson insisted they keep the doors locked. In the end the doors stayed locked, Wilson stayed not shot and the pair left empty-handed. But Wilson remembered what Troy looked like and later identified him in court, where the crim was sentenced to transportation.

And so in 1811, Troy arrived in Sydney Cove on the Providence with 77 other convicts. It took a few years but, in 1816, he came to be assigned to James Squire to do some work around the house. As he would soon find out, Squire was a handy friend to have.

The following year Troy was a free man, though he continued to work with Squire. In 1818, he tightened the link with Squire by marrying Elizabeth Smith. Her sister Jane was the wife of Francis Spencer, Squire's first Australian-born offspring, which made Troy brother-in-law with one of Squire's kids.

This link with the rich man of the region was helpful when Troy's house was robbed on July 26, 1820. In the dead of night, two men entered the home of Patrick and Elizabeth and stole three gold rings, a pair of gold ear-rings, a new shawl, quite a few yards of various cloth, three shirts, two pairs of women's cotton stockings, Troy's certificate of freedom and a whole lot of other stuff. We know this because Squire's reward notice in the *Sydney Gazette* just days after the break-in was very detailed.

In that same notice, Squire promised the not-insubstantial sum of £5 to "whoever will give such information as may lead to the apprehension and conviction of the desperadoes".

Despite the offer of a reward, the "desperadoes"

were not quickly apprehended. Lawrence Murphy and Daniel Keane were at large for six months before being caught with Troy's property in hand and being put on trial in January 1821. The pair offered an exceptionally weak defence – "we didn't steal anything guvner, we found all this stuff". Obviously, the court didn't buy that for a second, sentencing them to corporal punishment and a three-year stretch in Newcastle.

So Troy got his stuff back and maybe, just maybe, Squire got to hold onto his £5.

39
Give it Away

*In which James Squire decides what do
with all his stuff*

It's early in 1822. Squire is 67 years old, which is not
a bad innings for the era. It's certainly longer than he
could have expected to live had he stayed in England.

But he's not feeling the best. As the weeks go on he
starts to feel more poorly, and spends more and more
time in bed. His partner Lucy looks after him as best
she can, while also having to oversee the running of
Squire's businesses.

Squire, a man who spent most of his life in this new
colony keeping busy, can't abide having to stay in bed.
It feels lazy, and on top of that it's always been hard
for him to lie comfortably due to the scars on his back
from those 300 lashes almost 30 years ago.

The scars are always covered by a shirt when he's in
public, and that allows others to forget where he came

from. It lets them overlook that this prosperous king of Kissing Point was once a lowly convict who was spat out of England and travelled to this strange place in the bowels of a ship, surrounded by others just like him.

Others may forget his convict past, but Squire doesn't, especially when he feels those scars catch against the linen of his shirt, or scrape the bedsheets at night. Lucy and the others before her would run their hand over his back, as if to show that the marks did not bother them. But they *did* bother him.

He knows that being a convict and being sent here was a blessing in disguise. It did cost him all hope of ever seeing his dear wife Martha and their children John, James and Sarah again. Even though he was halfway around the world, destined never to see Martha again, he still couldn't bring himself to marry another. But the seven-year sentence to Sydney Cove also gave him boundless chances that would have never been open to the likes of him in England.

It's hard for him to imagine anyone in England carrying scars of a convict across their back ever being allowed to climb even a rung or two up the social ladder as he has here. In Sydney, he's managed to climb enough of those rungs that others now look up to him, and even the colonial leaders have been known to utter his name – and in admiration, not disgust.

But he also knows those scars to be a curse, a permanent reminder he carries of just where he came from and what he's done. Those scars are something best worn by a convict and not a pillar of the community. Perhaps the community has forgotten about them, but he hasn't. Those days in late 1789 when he was twice tied to that pole and whipped – 150 lashes each time – are always with him. Just like those scars.

By March, the illness has not abated. If anything, Squire feels worse, more lethargic. Getting out of bed is far too much of a chore. The doctor comes round and suggests he has cancer. Squire knows enough about medicine to know that's not a good sign. Yet, still he hopes he might see signs of improvement. I've come this far already, he thinks, surely a few more years isn't too much to expect.

A month later and he realises that, perhaps a few more years is unlikely. The way he feels, a few more months might also be unlikely. If he were to die this year, he does notice it would bring a strange symmetry – it would split his life almost in half. There would be the 34 years he spent in England, and then there was almost the same amount of time in Sydney. How appropriate, he thinks to himself, that the journey in a convict ship in 1787-88 should come to so neatly split his life half.

He knows it's time to get his affairs in order. He feels proud of what he's achieved here and how many possessions he has to pass on to various loved ones and those who aided him.

So around April 6, he begins to write (or dictates to someone else) a six-page document that starts with the words; "This is the last will and testament of one James Squire of Kissing Point …"

There is a chance that Squire's last months passed something like that. But perhaps they didn't – we'll never really know for sure. But he most certainly left a will, one in which he seemed to have managed to bequeath something to each member of his larger-than-normal family.

He could have ended up with fewer assets to divvy up. In May 1817, he placed an ad in the *Sydney Gazette*, putting all the land he owned up for sale, as well as 100 Merino ewes, six heifers and a bull. Why he chose to sell up isn't known for sure, but there is the suggestion that he was looking to shack up with Lucy Harding at her place and therefore no longer had a need for all this land. Or maybe he felt he was just too old and wanted to pack it all in.

While it may not be clear why he wanted to sell, what is clear is that he wanted to sell all of it. And to the one buyer; there is no indication that he would entertain the possibility of selling it off in bits and pieces – it was all or nothing. It seems a big ask to find one person who has both an interest in all of Squire's land and who is cashed-up enough to be able to afford it all. So maybe Squire's heart wasn't completely in the sale.

He did try and sweeten the pot a little bit – any buyer would also take home "300 weight of hops" from the latest harvest.

Five years later, all this land and sundry animals appear in his will, so either Squire could not find that one magic buyer or he had a change of heart and decided to keep it all.

And so he writes his own will. Or he dictates it to someone else. It's hard to conclusively state one way or the other, which is a real shame because if we knew for sure it was in his own hand it would be the longest document Squire wrote that we still have and it would speak volumes about his level of education.

The problem is that, aside from that day in June 1793 where he witnessed a convict wedding and signed his name on the marriage certificate, there are no other documents definitely written in his own hand.

In favour of Squire writing his own will is that it is in the first person. Also, the way his own name is signed at the end of the will is largely identical to the way he writes his son James Squire's name in the body of the will – only the J is different, which suggests they were written by the same person.

In favour of it being in some unknown person's hand is the fact that what is meant to be Squire's signature at the bottom of the will doesn't really resemble his signature from that marriage certificate. There is a "JS in brackets immediately after Squire senior's name so perhaps the man himself just initialised what someone else wrote. That would also explain why the names of James Squire senior and junior look very similar – they were both written by the same unknown person.

Also against it being in his own hand is the section at the end of the will that names the witnesses. That is written in the same hand as the body of the will and is in the first person – from the perspective of the witnesses ("… for his last will and testament in the presence of us…"). This would seem to count against the theory that because the body of the will is written from Squire's perspective, therefore it must be in his hand.

One other thing; if Squire was ill at the time of the

will being written (cancer is the illness that most have claimed he had) then the writing seems quite neat and ordered to have come from the pen of someone who was about to shuffle off this mortal coil. The words are neat and evenly spaced and sentences go straight across the page, which is no mean feat on unlined paper. That the ill Squire could write like that for the six pages of his will does seem unlikely.

So as much as I'd have liked it to be otherwise I have to conclude that he didn't write the will himself.

That said, there are still a number of valuable things to be drawn out of James Squire's will. Firstly, despite not having seen his wife Martha and their children for more than 30 years, Squire didn't forget them. He left Martha £50, the equivalent of more than £10,000 today. His English children John, James and Sarah each got £30.

The Sydney-born James (whose mother was Elizabeth Mason) was named an executor for the will – alongside Squire's partner Lucy Harding. In the will he scored the brewery and house at Kissing Point as well as the 25 acres they stood on. But that wasn't all – he also got another three land lots, bringing his tally to 221 acres.

James' sister Elizabeth landed 170 acres as well as Squire's house in Castlereagh Street while Mary Mason appears to have been the favoured child, being left four land lots totalling a whopping 950 acres.

All of which makes you feel sorry for their sister, Priscilla. She was the one whose father was listed as Phillip Morris on her birth certificate. In the will, Squire admitted paternity, calling her "a natural daughter of mine by the said Elizabeth Mason" – the same words used to describe all the other children they had together. However, her share of her father's assets paled into insignificance when compared to her siblings; she was left with just 30 acres of land to hold until her son James Devlin turned 21 and then *he* got it. So she really got nothing to call her own.

It really causes one to wonder at the relationship between Squire and Priscilla. Did she do anything during her life to cause her father to divide the riches in such a way that she effectively missed out altogether? Or perhaps the paltry amount she was left was because he was not really her father. Had Elizabeth fallen pregnant to the mysterious Phillip Morris early in her relationship with Squire? Did Squire reluctantly choose to raise the baby Priscilla as one of his own, leaving her less in his will than her siblings because she wasn't a "real" daughter of his?

The grossly uneven split of the loot among Elizabeth Mason's kids certainly raises a few questions and serves to increase the mystery of just who Priscilla's father was.

Squire's first Australian son Francis (whose mother, Mary, had died) got £30, as did John Bray, the son of Squire's deceased daughter Martha Mason.

Sarah Mason was left £100 and her son George Lucas (not that one, another one) got £30.

Someone by the name of Mary Audling got £100 and "a suit of mourning" for services to his family while five other servants got just £10 to buy their own mourning suit.

Squire certainly didn't forget his current partner Lucy. In terms of liquid assets, she was the big winner, being left £900. She also got a boat that bore her name, the bed and bedstead they slept in "and any other articles of household furniture she may choose amounting in value with those already mentioned to the sum of £100".

Whatever was left over was to be divided up between the Mason kids – which the will stated included Priscilla. As is so often the case with a parent's will, the kids would soon start squabbling over it. The legal fight was apparently sparked by some dubious antics from executor James Squire Jr, which we will read about soon.

<u>40</u>
The End

In which we say goodbye to James Squire

On the evening of Thursday, May 16 – "after an illness of about three months", according to the *Sydney Gazette*, James Squire drew his last breath. Where he was we don't really know but it seems a safe bet to say he was at home with his partner Lucy.

Eight days later, the *Gazette* prints an obituary full of praise. But, really, how often do you see an obituary that gives the dead person a good kicking? Well, there was that total hatchet job the *Gazette* did on Bennelong, but aside from that one.

"As one of the primary inhabitants of the colony, having come hither in the First Fleet in 1788, none ever more exerted himself for the benefits of the inhabitants than the deceased," the obituary stated.

"He was the first that brought hops to any perfection and hence was able to brew beer of an excellent quality. 'Squire's beer' was well-known.

"He might for long residence be styled the patriarch of Kissing Point as he lived where he died, 26 years."

Incidentally, that reference to hops is the first time Squire is spoken of as being the first to grow hops. Maybe it's true, maybe it's a case of an obituary gilding the lily a bit.

The obituary closes by lamenting that "by the frequent visitation of death", the First Fleeters "are becoming thinned in their ranks".

"This should lead to reflection, for the day will soon arrive when even those, now living, shall cease to say 'I came in the First Fleet'."

There are references today that claim Squire's funeral was the biggest the colony had seen. That may well be the case but I could find no contemporary reference to it. The *Sydney Gazette* made no mention of it, which would seem odd for such a large event, and one marking the passing of such a highly-thought-of citizen.

Squire's body was placed in the soil at the Devonshire Street Cemetery. Years later, in June 1901, the *Sydney Truth* newspaper visited the cemetery and wrote a story about the relocation of its coffins and tombstones to make way for Central train station. This is good news for us because the *Truth* journalist noticed Squire's memorial had not yet been removed. These days it seems the exact whereabouts of Squire's headstone is unknown, but this journalist saw fit to jot down the words carved into it – "Sacred to the memory of James Squire late of Kissing Point, who died May 16, 1822. He arrived by the First Fleet, and by integrity and industry acquired and maintained an unsullied reputation. Under his care the hop plant was first cultivated, and in this settlement he created the first brewery, which progressively matured to perfection."

A photo taken of the grave site marker shows the journalist left out the last paragraph, which read "as a father, a husband, a friend and a Christian, he lived respected and died lamented". The same marker also mentions his son James Jr, who died a few years later. So maybe father and son lay in the same grave.

Squire had been in the ground for almost two years before the children started to squabble over who got what in the will. On April 29, 1824, Lucy Harding posted a notice in the *Gazette* that suggests the other executor of the will, James Squire Jr, was being a bit shady.

In her notice Harding "hereby cautions the public against purchasing any property belonging to the estate of the late Mr James Squires [interesting how that S has returned to the end of his name], of Kissing Point, deceased, from a person of the name of James Mason alias Squires; he having no authority whatever to dispose of the same."

While the notice did not state what Squire Jr was trying to flog off, one could safely assume it was from the remainder of his dad's assets, which the will stated were to be shared equally among the children.

This action may well have led to Squire Jr's sisters Priscilla, Mary and Elizabeth taking both he and Harding to court in July 1824 for collecting money owed to the estate and flogging things off without telling them.

"[The executors] proceeded to collect in all the outstanding debts due to the estate and to make sale of part of the real and personal estate of the testator [aka James Squire] of very considerable value without rendering to your petitioners any account whatever although they have on various occasions made applications to James Squire and Lucy Harding to render the accounts …"

Squire Jr provided the accounts by late July 1824 and the sisters must have been happy with the numbers because they do not appear to have taken the matter any further.

41
Bodies

In which it is suggested James Squire had a surprising effect on beer from beyond the grave

Squire's brewery lived on for more than a decade after his death. James Jr took over the operations in 1823 and reportedly pumped out a decent amount of beer until he joined his dad in the ground in 1826. If James Jr's obituary in the *Sydney Gazette* was anything to go by, he wasn't missed as much as his dad. On March 11 the paper reported "DEATH – On Sunday last, Mr James Squire of Kissing Point. The deceased was much respected". The shortness of the obituary really leaves one thinking that maybe he wasn't that well respected at all.

At the very least a convict named Hans Peebles didn't respect him. In September that year Hans was busted stealing one of the late James' beer casks. A fellow brewer spotted him rolling it down the street. Hans claimed it had been in his house for ages and had just been wheeling it to a cooper for repairs when he was spotted. The court didn't believe a word of it and sentenced him to 28 days on the treadmill. And not like a treadmill in the gym either; rather it was a large, long rotating cylinder used to crush grain. Convicts would power the cylinder's rotation by walking on it all day – 40 minutes on and a 20-minute break – and with the risk of being mangled in the machinery if their foot slipped.

The brewery didn't reopen again until 1828, when Squire Sr's son-in-law Thomas Farnell (who had married Squire's daughter Mary) took over. He placed a notice in the *Sydney Gazette* to let people know the brewery and hotel were back in business. "TC Farnell will spare no pains or expense, in order to supply his friends with good wholesome beer, not to be excelled by any house in the colony."

Having just spoken of the quality of the beer, Farnell followed it up with this somewhat arrogant remark, "The above brewery is too well known for the quality of its beer, to need any further comments."

A year later, Farnell seems to have changed the name of the Malting Shovel Tavern to The Adventurer. A list of licenced publicans in *The*

Australian shows Farnell's premises in Kissing Point as having that name.

By 1834, Farnell too was in the ground; the *Sydney Herald* reported he died aged 34. "His remains were followed to the grave by nearly the whole of the brethren of the three Masonic Lodges of Australia, and a great number of private friends."

Two people had taken over Squire's operations and both of them died a few years after they started brewing – it's enough to make you wonder if the place was cursed.

While this may have been the case (hint: it probably wasn't), James Squire wasn't quite done with making beer. There's a chance that he was involved in a beer almost 100 years after his death. And I mean "involved" quite literally.

Squire was interned in the Devonshire Street cemetery. You can't go there anymore because Central station is there. In 1901, the government took back the cemetery to build the station, giving descendants two months to remove the bodies and take them elsewhere. Squire's body ended up going to Botany Cemetery where, according to a footnote in David Hughes' journal article 'Australia's First Brewer', his headstone "cannot now be identified".

But while the Devonshire Street Cemetery was in

the centre of town, it was a pretty crappy area – even as cemeteries go. In 1878, the *Illustrated Sydney News* called for work to improve the drainage in the area "to carry the essence of decayed humanity into the harbour sewers, or to remove the brick and stone buttress in Elizabeth Street, through which slimy and offensive matter oozes after rainy weather".

Now almost across the road from the place leaking "decayed humanity" was the Albion Brewery. And guess where the brewery got its water? According to David Clark's essay on the Sydney water supply "Sydney's pollution problems are alleged to have actually improved the taste of the local beer. The Albion Brewery's water reservoir received the drainage from the Devonshire Street Cemetery and the beer it produced had a distinctive flavour, later found to be a product of the pollution".

So it's possible some of James Squire found its way into the Albion Brewery's water supply and from there into their patrons' beer glasses. Cheers!

Bibliography
Every Day I Write the
Book

*In which the author gives a shout-out to a
lot of other books he read*

Chapman, Don, *1788 The People of the First Fleet*,
Doubleday, 1981

Clark, David 'Worse than Physic - Sydney's Water
Supply 1788-1888' in Kelly, Max (ed), *Nineteenth-
Century Sydney*, Sydney History Group, 1978

Cobley, John, *Sydney Cove 1788*, Angus and
Robertson, 1962

Cobley, John, *Sydney Cove 1789-1790*, Angus and
Robertson, 1963

Cobley, John, *Sydney Cove, 1791-1792*, Angus and
Robertson, 1963

Cornell, Martyn, *Amber, Gold and Black – The History of
Britain's Great Beers*, The History Press, 2010

Deutsher, Keith M, *The Breweries of Australia*, Beer & Brewer Media, 2012

Duff, Eamonn, 'Found: Long-lost grave of Bennelong, *Sydney Morning Herald*, March 20, 2011

Duff, Eamonn, 'Finding Bennelong', *Sunday Age*, March 27, 2011

Duff, Eamonn, Bennelong's remains too fragile to disturb', *Sun Herald*, September 18, 2011

Frost, Alan, *Botany Bay – The Real Story*, Black Inc, 2012

Frost, Alan, *The First Fleet – The Real Story*, Black Inc, 2011

Fullagher, Kate, ''Bennelong in Britain, *Aboriginal History*, Volume 33, ANU Press

Geeves, Philip, *A Place of Pioneers*, Ryde Municipal Council, 1970

Gillen, Mollie, *The Founders of Australia: A Biographical Dictionary of the First Fleet*, Library of Australian History, 1989

Gilling, Tom, *Grog: A Bottled History of Australia's First 30 Years*, Hachette Australia, 2016

Hill, Jennifer, Gibson, Elizabeth and Woodward,

Theodora, *Heritage Report for Halvorsen's Boat Yard*, Architectural Projects Ltd, August 7, 2014

Historical Records of Australia, Series I, Volume I 1798-1796, The Library Committee of the Commonwealth Parliament, 1914

Historical Records of Australia, Series I, Volume II 1797-1800, The Library Committee of the Commonwealth Parliament, 1914

Historical Records of Australia, Series I, Volume III 1801-1802, The Library Committee of the Commonwealth Parliament, 1915

Historical Records of Australia, Series I, Volume IV 1803-June, 1804, The Library Committee of the Commonwealth Parliament, 1915

Historical Records of Australia, Series I, Volume V July 1804-August 1806, The Library Committee of the Commonwealth Parliament, 1915

Historical Records of Australia, Series I, Volume VI August 1806-December 1808, The Library Committee of the Commonwealth Parliament, 1916

Historical Records of Australia, Series I, Volume IX January 1816-December 1818, The Library Committee of the Commonwealth Parliament, 1917

Historical Records of Australia, Series I, Volume X January 1819-December 1822, The Library Committee of the Commonwealth Parliament, 1917

Holden, Robert, *Orphans of History: The Forgotten Children of the First Fleet*, Text Publishing, 1999

Hughes, David, 'Australia's First Brewer', *Journal of the Royal Australian Historical Society*, Volume 82, Part 2, December 1996

Hughes, Robert, *The Fatal Shore*, Vintage, 2013

Humphries, Glen, *The Slab: 24 Stories of Beer in Australia*, Beer is Your Friend Publications, 2017

Hunt, David, *Girt: The Unauthorised History of Australia Volume I*, Black Inc, 2013

Hunt David, *Girt: The Unauthorised History of Australia Volume II*, Black Inc, 2016

Karskens, Grace, *The Colony – A History of Early Sydney*, Allen & Unwin, 2009

Keneally, Thomas, *Australians: A Short History*, Allen & Unwin, 2016

Keneally, Thomas, *Australians: Origins to Eureka*, Allen & Unwin, 2009

Keneally, Thomas, *The Commonwealth of Thieves*, Random House Australia, 2005

Levell, David, *Tour to Hell*, University of Queensland Press, 2008

Lindsay, Patrick, *True Blue: 150 Years of Service and Sacrifice of the NSW Police Force*, HarperCollins, 2012

McKenna, Mark, *The Captive Republic: A History of Republicanism in Australia 1788-1996*, Cambridge University Press, 1996

Moore, Judith, *The Appearance of Truth: The Story of Elizabeth Canning and Eighteenth-Century Narrative*, New Jersey Associated University Presses Inc, 1994

Mundle, Rob, *The First Fleet*, ABC Books, 2014

Old Bailey Online (oldbaileyonline.org), Mary Squires, Susannah Wells, Violent Theft, robbery, February 21, 1753

Parsons, TG, 'The Limits of Technology or Why Didn't Australians Drink Colonial Beer in 1838', *Push From the Bush*, Volume 4, 1979

Parsons, TG, 'Was John Boston's Pig a Political Martyr?', *Journal of the Royal Australian Historical Society*, Volume 71, Part 3, December 1985

Smith, Keith Vincent, 'Bennelong among his people', *Aboriginal History*, Volume 33, ANU Press

Sydney Gazette, various editions 1804-1822

Unknown, 'Devonshire Street Cemetery', *Sydney*

Truth, June 23, 1901

Unknown, *James Squire/s – The Remarkable Life of Australia's First Brewer*, Fellowship of First Fleeters – Hunter Valley chapter website

White, John, *Journal of a Voyage to New South Wales*, 1790

Can't Stop the Music

If you have any semblance of pop culture knowledge you've probably noticed that all the chapters in this book carry song titles. Which, on the one hand, is a bit dumb, because it's totally anachronistic – it's not like Squire ever sat down and listened to The Clash or Jane's Addiction. But on the other hand, coming up with chapter titles is a pain in the butt. And using song titles was just a lot more fun. Though also tricky; trying to find popular songs that somehow relate to the life of a man who was 50 years in the ground before Edison invented the gramophone wasn't always a breeze.

It started out by chance, with chapter two. The lyric "I'm a dandy highwayman" from Adam and the Ants' *Stand and Deliver* got stuck in my head when I was writing that chapter and so I used it. Soon enough, the idea became to use song titles for each chapter.

Kudos to you if you recognised every single song title in the book. I reckon you'd be very much in the minority. For the majority of readers, to save you having to Google each title (because it's likely annoying you that you can't figure some of them out) I've included a list of each title and where the song came from.

Because I'm a tops guy like that.

A Note to the Reader - Hello

What better way to start off a book by saying "Hello"? This is of course Lionel Richie's hit from his 1983 album *Can't Slow Down*. It's perhaps best remembered as the inspired selection for the Tap King ad. Or maybe because the original video features a blind woman managing to make a surprisingly accurate bust of Lionel Richie despite not being able to see. Also, can we just pause for a minute and contemplate the tackiness of having a blind woman in the video, when the song includes lyrics like, "is it me you're looking for?". Lionel, she's blind, she can't "look" for anything.

Another Note to the Reader - Hello Again

Okay, having two notes to the reader caused me a headache for ages in terms of coming up with a song title. And then I remembered The Cars' *Hello Again*, released in 1984. I was living in the United States when the song – and album *Heartbeat City* – came out. And I hated it. And hated The Cars too. Still do – so many of their songs sound like cheesy pop made for six-year-olds.

Introduction - Let's Go

This is one precisely two Cars songs that I don't hate (the other being *Just What I Needed*). Even though "She's winding them down, on her clock machine" is such a stupid lyric. You just meant "clock", didn't you? But you wanted a rhyme for "seventeen" in the next line, so you came up with "clock machine" – a phrase that no one has ever used outside this song. When someone asks the time, no-one answers by saying "hey, look at the clock machine on the wall".

1. We're a Happy Family

The original title for this was *Running in the Family*, a 1987 hit in Australia from UK's Level 42. Never heard of them? Yeah, that's why I changed the title – well that and the fact the song is terrible. Much better to go with a Ramones song. And I've always found the placement of that "Daddy likes men" line amusing.

2. Stand and Deliver

This comes from the two-year spurt of fame for

Adam and the Ants, the band that made having two drummers and a horizontal stripe of white paint across the bridge of your nose briefly cool. *Ant Music* is still a good song too. "That music's lost its taste, so try another flavour" is a great lyric.

3. I Don't Like Mondays

The song was written after Bob Geldof heard about 16-year-old Brenda Ann Spencer's shooting a gun in a kids' playground, killing two adults and injuring eight children and a cop. She said she did it because "I don't like Mondays. This livens up the day". But these days it's more of an FM radio staple, which is played – you guessed it – on a Monday morning as people head to work. Because people hate heading to work on Mondays, geddit?

4. Jailhouse Rock

Come on, you had to know this was an Elvis Presley song. Don't force me to think less of you.

5. Six Months in a Leaky Boat

Yes, I'm aware the First Fleet took a little more than six months to sail from England to Sydney. I'm just taking a bit of artistic licence here. Besides, if I recall correctly, this Split Enz song is more of a metaphor for the depression of songwriter and singer Tim Finn that anything nautical.

6. When Will I Be Famous

This is from Bros, the trio that featured the Goss twins and some other guy who wasn't related. Which kinda ruined the whole "Bros" name thing and maybe gave the third guy an inferiority complex ("why didn't they include me in the band name?"). And the answer to the question posed by the song title? "For a short period of time in 1987 and then the readers of *Smash Hits* will find some other teeny crap to listen to".

7. Taking Care of Business

Yeah, it's Bachman-Turner Overdrive with the one song of theirs people actually know. Which meant they probably had to play it at the end of each gig because people would leave afterwards.

"Hey, they played that business song - let's go home now."

"But wait, they haven't played *You Aint Seen Nothing Yet.*"

"Huh?"

"You know, 'B-b-b-baby you aint seen nnn-nothing yet'."

"That's them too. Wow, I know TWO of their

songs."

8. Let's Talk About Sex

Perhaps the best-known hit from that seasoned duo Salt-N-Pepa. Geddit? Seasoned – because they're salt and pepper. Okay, never mind. Funny thing, for a song that professes to talk about sex, they don't actually talk about sex that much. It starts with a chorus and then the first verse is all about how they're going to talk about sex. And up comes the chorus again, promising that we'll talk about sex. Then more than a minute into the song they actually talk about sex in the second verse. Until the chorus comes back and then they wonder if it'll get played on the radio and then we're back into the chorus again. The third verse brings a bit more sexy talk. But then, for the last minute of the song it's that frigging chorus again. Seems they spend more time telling us how they're going to talk about sex than, you know, actually talking about sex.

9. Hang Around

This comes from Wollongong's own Tumbleweed and is the opening cut on their 1995 *Galactaphonic* album. Forget *Sundial* or *Daddy Long Legs*, it's *Hang Around* that is the band's best tune as far as I'm concerned. Though I'm buggered as to why the video features them being chased around the city by a big chicken.

10. Been Caught Stealing

Didn't like Jane's Addiction at the time. And I still don't now. But I couldn't go past the song title for this chapter. You know, 'cause James Squire was caught stealing.

11. Smallpox Champion

From Fugazi, the most indie of indie bands. Back when was I younger and ran a music webzine (which is what we called blogs back then) one of my favourite moments was scoring an interview with them. This brutal piece of work sits on their *In On The Kill Taker* album.

12. Police and Thieves

Not the Junior Murvin version – which is really light and poppy for a song about police brutality – but The Clash's effort. That one is more pointed and edgy, especially with the sharp, cutting guitar riff throughout the song. Much better in my opinion.

13. Whip It

My daughter is at the age now where she likes to see

music videos of the songs from when I was growing up. I started playing this one by Devo and about 10 seconds in I remembered the whole video is basically about a guy whipping a girl tied to a post until all her clothes come off. I wasn't keen on the sort of conversation that would spark and so I quickly found another video. I watched the whole thing later on and was struck by just how unpleasantly misogynistic it seems to modern eyes.

14. The Dead Heart

It's from Midnight Oil - and I figure Arthur Phillip had to have a bit of a dead heart to think kidnapping the natives was a good idea.

15 Sweet Child O' Mine

I'm not often the guy who gets into a band way before everyone else. And sometimes I can miss the boat entirely. Guns N' Roses are a case in point. I wanted nothing to do with the mega-selling album *Appetite For Destruction* because I thought they were a bunch of poseurs. Not just Axl, all of them. Of course, I eventually caught up and bought *Use Your Illusion II* (because of *The Terminator II* song *You Could Be Mine*) but by then it was a bit too late.

16. Gimme Head

I was a bit of a fan of The Radiators in the 1980s – had their first five albums. Back then the idea of a song blatantly about getting blowjobs seemed very naughty, prompting infantile giggles. Now, the nature of the song seems pretty tacky, especially when a number of their other songs show they could write a pretty decent pop song.

17. I Fought the Law

Originally recorded by Sonny Curtis when he joined The Crickets in 1960, they did it with a country tinge. Then in 1966 the Bobby Fuller Four came along and re-recorded it – which is the version most of us know. But I had The Clash's version in mind, partially because – unlike the previous versions – at least The Clash looked like people who would actually get in trouble with the law.

18. No Word From China

Back in the late 1980s, I found a double-album companion to Stuart Coupe and Glenn A Baker's book *The New Rock N Roll*. It had songs from loads of bands I'd never heard before – The Fleshtones, Payolas, The Birthday Party and a postpunk band from

Newcastle called Pel Mel. They're the ones behind the song *No Word From China*. It's angular, slightly odd and pretty much the only song from that double LP that still pings round my head to this very day.

19. The Imposter

This corker of a song comes from Elvis Costello and appears on his 1980 album *Get Happy!!* (though I first heard it on the Concert for the People of Kampuchea live album) Three years later Costello would use The Imposter as a pseudonym to release the anti-Thatcher tune *Pills and Soap* and his next backing back after The Attractions would be The Imposters. So he got a bit of mileage out of that song title.

20. Sign Your Name

Just because they're used as chapter titles doesn't mean I like all these songs. This is a case in point – this Terence Trent D'Arby song was picked solely because it's the first song I could think of that referred to someone signing their name. Besides, Terence looks like the third member of Milli Vanilli, which is never a good thing.

21. More Than a Feeling

It's a song performed by Boston, on a chapter

about John Boston. Clever, huh? It's also the song from which Kurt Cobain snaffled the guitar riff for *Smells Like Teen Spirit*. So I guess Corporate Rock might still suck – but, hey, it's okay to swipe from it.

22. First in Line

I first heard this tune from The Romantics as the B-side (remember those?) to their huge single (remember those, too?) *What I Like About You*. It's on their debut album but it's what you'd technically refer to as "filler". I kinda feel sorry for those who bought the album on the strength of *What I Like About You*, because that's the strongest track.

23. Kill the Pig

The Tall Shirts were a weird, weird Australian band of the late 1980s. And I mean weird in terms of their music. It mashed up Hawaiian, gospel, swamp, blues, rock, rockabilly and whatever else they could get their hands on. A chapter about killing a pig can have no better song title that this effort. Go check out their live performance of the tune on YouTube. Strange cats indeed.

24. More Beer

Fear was a California hardcore punk band from the

late 1970s to early 1980s. This wasn't their best song but, when you're looking for songs about beer the pickings are slim. Basically it's a whole load of country and western songs and this one. I have to admit the Journey-style pisstake in the breakdown of this song is cool). Fear's best song? Well, that would be *Let's Have A War*, which manages to be smart, dumb and malevolent at the same time. How many punk songs namecheck the Dow Jones?

25. Get Free

This was going to be *I'm Free* by the Soup Dragons but I went back to watch the video and remembered how intensely I loathed that band. So I changed to this tune from The Vines.

26. The Stroke

US rocker Billy Squier is usually remembered for the cringeworthy video to *Rock Me Tonite*. And that's understandable – it features him dancing incredibly badly through a set done up to be a bedroom. It's like the video director said "yes, the song has the word "rock" in the title, but I want to act in the most un-rock way. Why? It'll seem ironic and clever". To his credit, Squier takes the mocking he cops for this video with good grace.

Once you've Googled that song, check out Squier's *The Stroke* – it's a bit more "rock".

27. Runaway

Because I'm old, I had Del Shannon's *Runaway* in mind when I came up with this chapter title. I wasn't aware of the Kanye West song *Runaway*. Nor The National's or Ed Sheeran's or The Kooks. But I did know of Bon Jovi's *Runaway* (check out the video – bad acting, bad hair, bad clothes). Yep, I'm so far behind the curve.

28. Strange Brew

While there is a great beer-related film with the same title, we're talking about the 1967 tune from Cream here. I'm no fan of the song – it just seemed to work with the chapter.

29. House of Fun

Like a lot of people, I thought for ages that this 1982 tune from Madness was actually about a house of fun. You know, like a fun park. But I was shocked to find out it was about a 16-year-old boy trying to buy condoms. Which obvious from a reading of the lyrics – which no radio or TV programmers must have done as it was played all over the place with no idea of the risque nature of tune. Well, in the '80s a song about a teenager buying condoms was risque.

30. I Will Follow

In my late 20s if I read a biography of a band, I suddenly became a fan of them and went out and bought their records. It was only ever a short-term thing – I didn't care for the band before reading the biography and, after a few months, it was as if I suddenly remembered that fact and quickly lost interest in the band.

Such was the case with U2 after reading *The Unforgettable Fire*. Went nuts for the band before waking up to myself and realising they were a bit wanky.

31. Hop, Skip, Jump

It's strange how some songs just get stuck in your head. I'd had the chorus to this song pinging around in there for ages. I'd told myself it was a song I'd heard on *Countdown* back in the early '80s. But I didn't believe myself, because the lyrics in my head included "Hop, skip, jump/Shake a leg" which are just too stupid to be from an actual song. Turns out it was an actual song – YouTube has New Zealand band The Orphans playing this. And I don't know why I remembered it for so long because it is an awful song. It was used for this chapter because "hop" is close to "hops".

32. Hey Stoopid

It's an Alice Cooper song about kicking drugs while also choosing not shoot yourself in the head. Seriously, go check out the lyrics.

33. Love Will Tear Us Apart

There are songs that you can sing along in your head for ages while being largely unaware of the true nature of the words. The Police's *Every Breath You Take* is a classic example – people think it's a love song but the lyrics are all about stalking someone.

While I knew the truth about The Police song I wasn't aware of just how goddamn dark the lyrics to the Joy Division song were until I had a look at them to write this bit. It's a tale of a deeply dysfunctional relationship and the words take on a deeper meaning when you consider the songwriter Ian Curtis committed suicide less than a year later. I'm not alone in missing that – the rest of Joy Division has since said they didn't twig to the cry for help that was in the lyrics.

I chose this for the chapter title about Squire's wife's death more for the general sadness of the song rather than any deeper meaning.

34. Go West

It's from the Pet Shop Boys. I never liked them. I just picked it because the song title worked with this chapter.

35. Peaches

Man, the lyrics to this song from The Presidents of the United States of America are so asinine: "Peaches come from a can, They were put there by a man, In a factory downtown". *Lump* is a far better song (and Weird Al's cover is better still) Can't believe they were nominated for a Grammy for this tune; though they didn't win. With The Beatles nominated in the same category (for that icky *Free as a Bird* tune), there was no way anyone else was going to win.

36. Don't Tear It Down

Ahh, Spy Vs Spy … I was such a huge fan of them back in the day. There aren't a lot of bands that can create a distinctive sound, one that is instantly recognisable. Spy Vs Spy was one of those bands. Even if you were hearing a song for the first time, you could pick it as a Spy song without any trouble.

37. Blackfella Whitefella

A mid-1980s tune from the Warumpi Band. Leaving aside the message of racial harmony, it's a damned catchy tune.

38. Friends

Andy Summers was lucky Sting was in The Police, because Andy's songs were always a little weird. Lyrically, at least. Musically, he managed to win a Grammy for Best Instrumental for *Behind My Camel*. This tune – the B-side to *Don't Stand So Close To Me* – is about cannibalism. Specifically eating your friends. It must have freaked out some of those teenage girls who bought the single.

39. Give It Away

It's a song from those noted purveyors of terrible lyrics, the Red Hot Chili Peppers. Here's a sample from this song "Realise I don't want to be a miser/Confide with sly you'll be the wiser". See, that doesn't mean anything.

40. The End

It's an appropriately-named tune for The Beatles, because it was the last song all four members would ever record together in a studio. *The End* is part of a medley of several short songs and contains the ironically uplifting lyric "And in the end, the love you take is equal to the love you make". It's ironic because the band would have an acrimonious break-up about five seconds after they left the studio.

41. Bodies

For a band prone to provoking outrage, the Sex Pistols didn't come up with that many truly outrageous songs. It was pretty much this one and *Belsen was a Gas* (though there was actually no gas chambers at the Belsen concentration camp). But *Bodies* is actually a pretty gross song – it's about a mentally ill friend of singer John Lydon who had an abortion and reportedly turned up to his house with the fetus in a plastic bag.

Bibliography – Every Day I Write the Book

It may surprise you to know that finding a song about books isn't easy. So thank you to Elvis Costello for writing one and having the Attractions perform it.

An Explanation – Can't Stop the Music

It's the title track from the Village People film of the same name. It features Steve Guttenberg as a songwriter/DJ, and the members of the Village People walk around in their stage costumes all the time, as though it's their usual attire. As an aside, I was only 10 when the Village People were huge and with God as my witness, I didn't realise there was a whole gay thing going on. I thought they were just five guys who liked to dress up in costumes.

Index – Five-Letter Word

An index is a list of words, so a song title that features the word "word" seems appropriate. And index is a five-letter word. Clever choice, huh? This comes from the sublime Australian power pop band The Numbers. Jeez, I don't know how these guys weren't huge.

Index
Five-Letter Word